RIDDLES OF NATURE

RIDDLES OF NATURE

Mahinder N. Gulati

GYAN

ISBN: 978-81-212-1281-6

Price: ₹ 750

First Published, 2015

Published by

Gyan Publishing House
23, Main Ansari Road
Daryaganj, New Delhi-110002
Phones: 23282060, 23261060
Fax : 91-11-23285914
E-mail: books@gyanbooks.com

Laser Typesetting: Awadhesh, Delhi

Printed at: G. Print Process, Delhi

Cataloging in Publication Data—DK
Courtesy: D.K. Agencies (P) Ltd. <docinfo@dkagencies.com>

Gulati, M. N., author.
Riddles of nature / Mahinder N. Gulati.
pages cm
Includes bibliographical references (pages).
ISBN 9788121212816

1. Nature—Psychic aspects. I. Title.

DDC 133.25 23

Contents

Preface

The last decade has witnessed volatility and turmoil in the Indian political scene such as was never seen before except during the times of "Emergency". The primary cause of this unfortunate trend has been exercise of supreme political authority without corresponding obligation of accountability, responsibility and transparency. It was this spectacle of political maneuvering and mismanagement that prompted me to pursue the line of thought that went into my latest work, *The Forgotten Political Avatar*, in order to press home the theme of clean politics, honest and corruption free governance supported by healthy investigative journalism—a positive much needed trend that was tragically cut short.

The genesis of my present work lies in a large number of stories, incidents, episodes, etc. — mostly authentic, spiced with some odd tales. These are stories of the mysterious, haunting, ghosts-apparitions, activities of the paranormal societies, excerpts from conversations by the 'mediums' with those on the "Other Side" normally referred to as the dead, numerous sightings reported in the media about UFOs and landings by aliens casting some doubts about the infallibility of Darwinian Theory of Evolution of Species, possibility of life on other planets and planetary systems, extra-terrestrial intelligence, *et al*. However, it was the NDE (Near Death Experience) and OBE (Out of Body Experience) and the amazing exploits of David Neal Alexandra, a French origin Lady Lama of Tibet, besides use of 'hypnotic regression' in treatment of mental ailments, *et al* that prompted me to put together all relevant material in a presentable format. Of course I do not claim any originality for the compilation. However, I accept full responsibility for indulging in my passion of ascribing spiritual-philosophical contents to those otherwise innocuous tales, as well as for any errors that might have crept in my interpretations during that process.

Although we have inherited a treasure house of philosophical-spiritual wisdom from our ancient scriptures, most modern literature on the subject comes from the West, as do most experimental works. This major transformation of the western thought process has come about primarily after the Tibetan Diaspora forced upon the sovereign independent nation.

Šrimad Bhagavadgitã is an excellent treatise on philosophy of life and death, life after death, birth and rebirth, law of karma, and so on. The very idea and concept that there is 'Life After death' has since been retrieved from the dustbins of spiritual philosophy and subjected to serious scientific studies to prove that **there is Life after Death**. More on this later ... Our scriptures like the Gita, Ramayana, Upanishads and the ancient wisdom of Puranas are in themselves a set of universities of philosophical knowledge and belief systems. It is unfortunate that most of our intellectual elite have kept themselves aloof from this modern trend. No doubt the Hindu missions of different hues have done a commendable job in furthering the spread of Indian thought, it is the Tibetan thought that has brought a whiff of fresh breeze to concepts like reincarnation, immortality of the soul, the meaning and nature of death, the same being merely a transitory phase rather than a terminus. However, Law of Karma has been an outstanding Indian (Hindu) contribution in this vast field.

After my retirement from the Army in 1978 I worked for about a decade in the Middle East on various project management assignments. This became a stepping stone for my 'Green Card' to become a permanent resident of California, USA which, in turn, facilitated my studies for my PhD from an Indian University. In the process the huge well stocked and catalogued libraries of Berkley and San Francisco Universities proved a vast store house of knowledge. The Bibliography at the end of this work speaks volumes about the value of rare out of print books to which I had access in Berkley University. I acknowledge with deep gratitude for having made liberal use of vast literature on subjects like paranormal phenomena, Para-Psychology, 'Near Death Experiences', 'Out of Body Experiences', Mysteries, Ghosts-Apparitions, Dreams, Séances communications with the Other Side via mediums, medical treatment via Regression, Reincarnation, Psychic Sciences, *et al.*

I trust the Bibliography at the end of this work would not only prove the point but also be useful to serious students of the subject.

1

Riddles of Nature

The genesis of this apparently fictitious, but unbelievably true narrative lies in a large number of stories of the mysterious, haunting, ghosts-apparitions, activities of the paranormal societies, excerpts from conversations by the 'mediums' with those on the "Other Side" normally referred to as the dead, numerous sightings reported in the media about UFOs and landings by aliens casting serious doubts about the infallibility of Darwinian Theory of Evolution of Species, possibility of life on other planets and planetary systems, extra-terrestrial intelligence, et al. However, it was the NDE (Near Death Experience) and OBE (Out of Body Experience), besides use of 'hypnotic regression' in treatment of mental ailments etc. that made me pickup and edit one of those innocuous but mysterious tales writtenby Pandit Shriram Sharma Acharya in his The Extra Sensory Potential of Mind published by Shri Vedmata Gyatri Trust, 2001, Haridwar. Although we have inherited a treasure-house of philosophical-spiritual wisdom from our ancient scriptures and saints, it is rather ironical that most of modern literature on the subject comes from the West, as do most experimental works. It is not that the West has suddenly developed intellectual-spiritual abilities out of their inherent wisdom; far from it! This major transformation of western thought process has come about generally out of impact of the Tibetan Diaspora besides selfless activities of Hindu missionaries during the 20th Century sans the Christian-Islamist proselytising persecution of those whom they call non-believers, contemptuously as infidels.

Notwithstanding the tremendous intellectual revolution in mankind, there still remain numerous kinks in the mysteries of nature which continue to demand a scientific explanation if at all there can be one. These continue to be Riddles of Nature. Just one small story to quote as an example:

Two families, Schulkoff and Hutten had gone to spend their summer holidays together on the Silt Island of the North Sea. After a week Hutten was called for emergency duty. When the rest of the party was returning to the camp site on August 02, 1923, the sea was calm and there were no indications of any stormy weather. However, all of a sudden there was terrible turbulence in the sea and Mr. Schulkoff noticed a huge boat fighting to survive the huge waves in the middle of the high sea. They also saw some fishermen on the shore trying to help their friends trapped in the deathly situation. They fired a cannon located on a stony platform to throw a 'life-line'. But the line was lost in the immense turbulent waves and did not reach the stricken boat. The visiting families were watching the entire saga in awe. The fishermen on shore made three more attempts to reach their comrades, but all in vain.

Meanwhile several fishermen, their families and children from the Colony had gathered on the shore. They were screaming in anguish and despair, praying for rescue. The tourist family also prayed for God's mercy. Concurrently, the naval security force was at site, attempting to rescue the fisherman striving for life in a deadly sea. Some naval cadets sailed in a small boat with emergency support. Slowly, they managed to reach the stricken boat. Unfortunately, before they could commence the rescue operation, a huge wave gulped the rescuers and the stricken boat. Within moments of the tragedy the sea became calm as if nothing had happened.

The tourists were in tears. They walked towards the place where the families had gathered but they too had mysteriously disappeared into the blues; no sign of any man, woman or child! Even the rest of the naval security guards were nowhere in sight. Nothing was there except the stony platform. The tourist family went to the stony platform and instead found a monument with the inscription on the platform:

"In the memory of the brave fishermen and their saviors who

Sacrifice their lives, fighting the dreaded cyclone on the eve of

2nd August 1872.

May their souls rest in peace"

Everyone in the tourist party was stunned, so were many others. Today was 2nd August! Was today's incident a replay of that tragic event of 1872? Everyone was puzzled. So they went over to the local priest and narrated the dreadful experience of the evening. He informed the congregation that the same mysterious experience occurs on the same day and time, every year. Thousands of detectives, scientists, police and public have experienced the same dreadful experience but there is yet no rational explanation for the mystery. In the words of Dr. Ramsey Bernard Hutten:-

"What all happens or is experienced in this world cannot be explained by the theories of science that is based on visible evidence. ... There is also a world beyond our perception and beyond the reach of our extrovert intellect, which cannot be grasped or sensed by any instrument. ..." Mind is an immense mine of potential power and mystery of which we are hardly aware of. This latent power source manifests itself from time to time bewildering us to no end. Right or wrong, it is very much there.

"We normally use only about 7 per cent of the real potential of our mind.... Noting the intrinsic and yet undeciphered cores of our mind, we should not have any prejudices in accepting the possibility that, if discovered and employed ingeniously, the science of the subliminal mind would elucidate the mysteries of nature and help enlighten the multiple dimensions of life with the glow of absolute truth." **— A quote by Sita Ram Sharma Acharya.**

So far so good: Agreed, the mind has immense hidden potential, perhaps still mostly untapped. However, the fundamental question still remains: What is mind? Where is it located in the body? How does it differ from the brain, or is it a part of the brain? What is the difference between human psyche and mind if at all these are different entities? So on and so forth. Indeed very valid questions, but these and allied questions are far too complicated and subtle, well beyond the scope of this work scope. For the present suffice is to say that while Empedocles of Agrigentium in 459 BC ascribed the individual psyche as a function of blood constituents, and Diogenes of Apollonian located the mind in the heart, Pythagoras was perhaps the first one to teach that brain is the primary seat of most mental activities. And if we bring the soul and Hindu philosophy into this discussion, the problem gets further compounded!

Incidentally, in Hindu cremation system a particular small bone having a distinct shape and size is particularly looked for, while collecting the ashes. It is called the atman (the soul) and kept apart for special treatment during the visarjan ceremony. However, Hindu philosophy lays emphasis on the soul being immortal, shapeless sans any physical characteristics. How do we reconcile to this contradiction? --- More about these mysterious Riddles of Nature later...

2

Xenoglossy

Past Life Recall

Xenoglossy (also Xenoglossia) is the ability to speak in an unlearned foreign language, usually based on past-life recall. It is a putative paranormal phenomenon and is of two types: 'Recitative' in which a person recites words or phrases of a foreign language without understanding their meaning; the second is the 'Responsive' type when a person is able to carry on a conversation in an unlearned language. For all practical purposes, xenoglossy is almost the same thing as "past life recall". The term was coined by Charles Richet around the turn of the 20th Century to distinguish the ability to know an unlearned foreign language from other traditional aspects of past-life recall phenomenon, more so because xenoglossy occurs extremely rarely while traditional past-life-recall phenomena are somewhat common occurrences.

The phenomenon of "Past Life Recall" is most common amongst young children between the ages of two to five. The mean age is about two-and-a-half-years. The phenomenon begins to taper off around age eight after which its appearance is indeed rare. This is as far as spontaneous recall is concerned. American parapsychologist and anthropologist, James Matlock, hypothesised that young children, particularly in non-Western societies, remember past lives more readily than adults because they are physically and psychologically less mature. As a person matures, past-life memories cannot easily penetrate the waking state.

Eastern cultures are immersed in mysticism and are more attuned to concepts of reincarnation and the law of karma. Naturally, past-life recall occurs in the East far more often than in Western societies. Past-life recall in adult life falls in the field of psychiatry and treatment of mental problems when recall is induced under hypnotic regression, yoga, bodywork etc. Spontaneous recall of past-life amongst young children has yielded impressive evidence in support of reincarnation but continues to lack scientific acceptance. Not only scientific proof of past life recall is lacking, it is also not clear whether the memories are of historical past, or are a reconstruction from the present subconscious mind. Moreover, there are instances of souls reincarnating together with each other over and over again. According to 'Yoga Sutras' compiled by Patanjali in A.D. 400 all details of past lives and all impressions of karma in the *chitta*, the subconscious mind, can be awakened through yogic meditation. Here I must mention that there have been several cases of spontaneous recall of past life reported from all over the world, besides the well documented case histories of Shanti Devi[1] and many others. However, the number and frequency from the Eastern societies are much higher than those from the West.

It is not only the children who have spontaneous past-life recall, the adults also do so. Numerous regression experiments over the recent past have shown that memories of past life are indeed a universal phenomenon. In fact, Dr. Ian Stevenson, Professor of

Psychiatry in the University of Virginia, has documented more than three thousand cases of verified reincarnations, a subject that used to be considered in exclusive domain of eastern spiritualism and Reincarnation-philosophy. He has shown that certain physical blemishes, or other birth marks, are sometimes carried over from one life to the next. In fact, Dr. Stevenson in his 1997-monumental work running into 2,268page and two volumes*Reincarnation and Biology: A Contribution to the Etiology of Birthmarks and Birth Defects* has documented more than 200 cases of birth-marks that corresponded with wounds on the deceased person whose life the children purported to recall. His Holiness the Dalai Lama and his family are a living proof of precisely this concept of transference of birth-marks from one life to next as an extension of principle of Reincarnation.[2]

Besides psychiatric regression, trans–hypnosis is another technique towards uncovering past-life recall. Swarnlata Mishra[3], a Hindu girl, born in 1948, is a classic case of recitative xenoglossy. This case was researched and documented in detail by Ian Stevenson in 1961.[4] — Between the ages of four and five, Swarnlata sang Bengali songs and performed Bengali dances without ever having been exposed to Bengali language or culture. She said she had been a Bengali woman in a previous life, and had learned the songs and dances from a friend. In this connection it is noteworthy that the earliest documented case of spontaneous past-life recall is that of a Japanese boy born in 1815 in a farmer's family. This boy had died at age six in 1810. He said that in his new present life till the age of four he remembered everything about his death, burial, Bardo-state (intermediate state between death and rebirth) and rebirth etc., till the age of four after which he could not recall his previous life.

In another case reported in 1862 by Prince Gallitzin, a mesmerist who magnetised an uneducated German woman. She told of a life in 18th Century France, and spoke French fluently. In her normal waking state she knew no French at all. In yet another case, a 37year old housewife, "T.E", was hypnotised by her physician husband. A series of sessions took place during 1955-56. The personality that emerged was that of "Jensen", a male peasant farmer who spoke an early form of Swedish in a deep masculine voice. He was never fluent, but spoke with some effort, sometimes repeating phrases almost automatically; otherwise he spoke in 17th Century colloquial Swedish. In Ian Stevenson's opinion T.E.'s ability to speak Swedish language was paranormal.

Two other instances on the same lines are those of Gretchen and Sharada, a Bengali-speaking woman who took over the life of Uttara Huddar, a Marathi-speaking Indian woman, on and off for at least eight years. Huddar, born in 1941, was 33 years old when Sharada manifested. In 1974 Huddar was hospitalised for a skin disease. In the hospital she followed the instructions of a visiting yogi who taught patients how to meditate. Huddar then began to suffer extreme mood swings and became a different person and identified herself as Sharada. But Sharada could converse only in Bengali, unknown to Huddar and her Family. Sharda apparently had died at age 23 during the first half of the 19th Century, but refused to believe she was dead. She periodically[4]

Stevenson Ian Pretyman, Dr.: Author of fourteen books on Reincarnation, including *Twenty Cases Suggestive of Reincarnation* (1966) besides more than 300 papers; *Where Reincarnation and Biology Intersect* (1977) His underlying theme was that certain phobias, unusual abilities and illnesses could not be explained by heredity or the environment. Instead, personality transfer via Reincarnation provided part of the answer.

Manifested for days, or even weeks at a time. Huddar and her family learnt to co-exist with the visiting personality out of sheer compulsion of life and its circumstances!

Xenography, the writing of an unlearned language, is even more difficult to verify than xenoglossy. Most likely it is the product of cryptomnesia as appears to have been the case a French medium who wrote long sentences in Greek. It was discovered that many of the sentences came from a French-Greek dictionary. However, Gretchen and Sharada wrote in German and Bengali respectively.

Head injuries resulting in unconsciousness, concussion accompanied by high fever often trigger past-life recall. The story of a three year old girl, Dorothy Louis Eady (alias Omm Sety: 1904-1981) is most fascinating. She was born of Irish parents in a London suburb in January 1904 and fell down a flight of stairs in England in 1907. She was pronounced dead but revived with no injuries. Soon after that she started dreaming of gardens and temples, and complained to her parents that she was not "home". Where was her home? She did not know! When she grew older she started believing that her "home" was in Egypt where she was a priestess sworn to virginity. She broke her vows and became the young illicit lover of Sety the First (1306 B.C.-1290 B.C.), a pharaoh in the Nineteenth Dynasty. In course of time she became pregnant with Sety's child and had committed suicide.

When Dorothy was old enough she studied archeology and Egyptology in English museums under some experts. The next phase: While still in her English home, Dorothy experienced 'Out-of-Body Experiences'

(OBE) during nocturnal dream state. During these trips Dorothy Eady would 'go over' to meet Sety on the "Other Side". In turn Sety's spirit would visit her at night. These romantic encounters with Sety via OBE continued. In 1930 she married an Egyptian citizen. She left her English home and family in 1954 and went to live in the primitive village of Arabet Abydos, the site of ruins of Sety's Temple. Here she pin pointed to archeologist engaged in excavation of ruins in the area the exact spot where to dig for Sety's ruins. She also predicted that there would be a tunnel running beneath the northern part of the Temple. Subsequent excavations proved her right, and that was most amasing indeed. Another more spectacular prediction was that underneath the Temple of Sety I,lies a secret vault containing a library of hidden historical and religious records. This too was verified as true.

Besides the foregoing, there are some other archeological claims regarding Sety's Temple which are yet to be verified. The Great Sphinx at Giza (Literally= Father of Dread) is the most outstanding one. It is a limestone statue of a reclining mythical creature with a lion's body and a human head believed to represent the face of Pharaoh Khafra. Omm Sety (Dorothy) believed that the Giza Sphinx does not represent the likeness of King Khafra as is conventionally believed the world over. In fact, it was built for the ancient Egyptian god Horus. Nevertheless, past life memories cannot be taken on face value and in some cases may be subject to fraudulent claims too.

While living in the primitive village surrounded by ancient ruins, Omm Sety came to believe that if she renewed her ancient priestess' vows of chastity and fealty, after her death she and Sety would be reunited forever, till eternity. Omm Sety (Eady) died in 1981 and is buried near Shunnet el-Zebib.

The essential element, the very basis of above episodes is the eastern Doctrine of REINCARNATION. Its fundamental principle is: Death is not a terminus; it is merely a passage from one state to another, then another and so on. All beings, humans and animals alike, are reborn after death — Humans as humans, or as animals, and vice versa. There is no life without death. "I am convinced that the lack of a physical body is my timeless natural state and existing with a physical body is as temporary as a dream ... Although I am on this earth, I am not of it. Moreover, I and we are incredible spiritual beings having a human experience, and not just humans having a limited human experience". Death must take place before a new life is born, in whatever form. "In each life the proportion of pain and joy which they experience is determined by their good and evil deeds in the life before, although they may modify that proportion by their efforts in their present life." The Hindus and Buddhists call this as the Law of Karma — Reap as you sow. However, karma is not a process that operates in nature; it operates in the human mind. It is our reaction to the circumstances, and not the circumstances themselves, that generate the karmic trace. Belief in rebirth is the principle element of faith on which Law of Karma holds its ground.

Law of Karma does not imply that a person has to accept whatever happens, happens because it was so ordained by fate. This is totally a negative interpretation of Karma. There is nothing to prevent a person from improving upon what fate is supposedly to have ordained. In fact it is within his/her power to improve upon one's existing condition — good, bad or indifferent.

Death is certain and Rebirth is inevitable: Bhagavad Gita (20)

The circumstances of next life are determined by the karmic traces of previous life. According to Tibetan belief system there are six possible realms into which an individual may take rebirth. In order of comfort these are: God Realm, the highest form; Demi-God Realm; the Human Realm; the Animal Realm; the Hungary Ghost Realm and the worst scenario are the Hell Realm. Anger is the root cause of Hell Realm which has eight hot and eight cold realms[5].

It is a strange belief system that denies the existence of God, or even a soul, although otherwise it is a highly spiritual belief system. However, the essence of the belief system is the Great Wheel of Birth, Death and Rebirth — a cycle that goes on and on ...

Live Experience of the Past

Live experience of past major events is entirely different from past life recall. In the former case the subject actually undergoes an experience as if he/she is either participating in the incident, or watching it live as if happening right in front of the senses.

Lieut. Col. David Smith of Gammery Town, England, published a report in a local newspaper sometime around 1900-01: "My son has a big farmhouse in Devon. It is situated far away from the town. The nearest house is about two km from here. One day, when my son was milking the cows behind the house at about 7:30 am, he heard loud sounds of

[5] Evans-Wentz W.Y.: The Tibetan Book of the Dead; Pilgrims Publishers, Varanasi, 1927; pp xxii, 236

Horse-tops. As though an army was marching nearby ... He could also hear the harsh jingling of weapons used in the earlier period of history. He thought it to be a part of shooting of a historical war-film. In order to get a clear view of the event, he came out of the compound to where his two servants were also present. But none of them could see anything. However, the noise was quite loud and clear as if hundreds of soldiers were sojourning through his house! The entire episode lasted for about an hour ..."

Some other persons too had similar experiences in the same region. Terrifying battlefield noises have also been heard from many parts of England and France. King Charles I had in fact got some cases investigated officially. The experiences of this type are often found in areas which were at sometime in the past were cantonments, battlefields or graveyards. In some cases soldiers, elephants, tents of their camps would be visible in the faint light of the evening. These episodes should not be discarded merely on scientific grounds. May be, these can be explained in the "fourth dimension of time beyond the three dimensional space in the periphery of our perception".

Time is not absolute. What is present goes into the past and what is yet to happen is supposed to exist in the future. But the seeds of the future are sown in the present. In the words of William Von-de-Venotz: "Every man and woman is endowed with the potential to arouse his inner intellect and see the future in the mirror of his mind." To quote an actual instance: The worst ever accident in American aviation history occurred on 26 May, 1979 when a DC-10 Jet of American Airlines crashed before landing inthe Chicago International Airport when all 275 on board were literally burnt into ashes. The accident was noted by David Booth an office manager in Cincinnati (Ohio) airport. He had a premonition of this tragic accident four days before the event on May 22, 1979 and had warned the Federal Aviation Authority and ground office of the Cincinnati Airport of his premonition. The inevitable happened; it had to.

Spiritual powers of the mind are not bound by the constraints of time and space; they are eternally liberated.

References

1. Sture Lunnerstrand (Author), Leslie Kippen (Translator) IHave Lived Before: The True Story of Reincarnation of Shanti Devi (and scores of others, more from the east than from western societies) Ozark Mountain Publishing, 1998 — The most thoroughly documented and authenticated case of Reincarnation in modern times in which Shanti Devi reveals extremely vivid memories of her experiences after Death, and later return to a physical body. Discover Reincarnation; Aquarian Press, 1992
2. His Holiness The Dalai Lama: My Land and My People; New Delhi 1977,
3. Guiley Rosemary Ellen: Encyclopedia of the STRANGE, MYSTICAL, and UNEXPLAINED; p. 655.

3

Stonehenge, Mehirs and Dolmen

Stonehenge is the most famous ancient Megalithic site in the world. It is pride of British heritage, a wonder of wonders. It means "Hanging Stones", literally so. The ancient megalithic marvel is located on the chalk-plain of Salisbury in Wiltshire, England. The giant circle of megaliths is made up of great uprights, more than 13 feet in height, called *sarsens*, each weighing nearly fifty tons. In the first place a huge circle was formed by installing thirty such monsters topped by huge lintels. The existing remains or ruins include a henge and a horseshoe arrangement of standing blue sandstones, having magical healing power, each weighing twenty-two tons apiece while the great uprights, the sarsens weigh fifty tons each. How on earth the ancient Saxons managed to carry such heavy stone columns and massive lintels all the way from the source in Ireland to the site and then hoist them into position high up in the air, and that too during the dark ages 3500 B.C. to 1100 B.C with none of the present day lifting-placing technological equipment — It is indeed an unimaginable marvel of human endeavour. May be, the spirits helped in building this medieval memorial, or as a healing center perhaps!

Inside this vast circle was another smaller one of sixty blue stones, each weighing about five tons; and inside this was a horse-shoe, also of blue stone. Another horse-shoe of five vast trilithons adds mystery to what may have been a Roman Temple built by the Druids. Astronomers suggest that it was meant to be a primitive crude structure designed to calculate dates of the eclipse, while archeologists believe that it was meant to honor the prehistoric peoples' ancestors. It is an icon of Great Britain, a spiritual place and a source of inspiration to the modern world. It is an enigma, indeed. Since it served a religious, social, political and astronomical function, Psychic powers were the inspiration for centuries of continuous hard labor. May be, Psychic Giants provided the labor force as is generally believed by the gullible.

Who built it? When? Why? There are different theories, speculations and the subject remains a fascination.

The megaliths were cut from outcrops of hard rock on the Marlborough Downs about twenty four miles from the site. The stones were then dragged on rollers or sleds for which a work force of about 1,500 powerful determined men was required, taking about two months for each stone to be transported. Perhaps it took about forty to fifty years, two generations or so, to merely transport the sixty huge heavy stones. At this stage the laborious task had just begun. Each stone had to be cut and shaped. Sarsens are extremely hard, so very hard that even the best of modern steel tools cannot dress and shape them. It took months to shape each stone. Now started the most dangerous and herculean part of the work --- to place the stones in a vertical position in the huge holes dug for the purpose and then to accurately align them thereafter. The lintels were the next equally arduous task! These were slid over on raised platforms and then position atop the tall vertical stones. Incidentally, the 5-tons blue stones numbering seventy-nine came from the nearest quarry about 135 miles away. What a stupendous undertaking in those primitive times! The builders had to rely on ropes, wooden rollers and plenty of manpower and the project are deemed to have been completed in 1500 B.C.E.

Fifty-six burial pits known as "Aubrey Holes" named after their discoverer contain bones of cremated humans, animal bones, flint, pottery, etc. It is believed that these holes served as entry points to the Underworld. At times portions of construction were left unfinished, dismantled and reconstructed over a period of centuries. The present form seems to have taken shape around 2000 B.C.

A British Astronomer Sir Norman Lock determined at the turn of the 20th century that Stonehenge was constructed to point to summer solstice. However, British Astronomer Gerald S. Hawkins, after computer calculations of 165 alignments of the stones with the sun and the moon, concluded in 1965 that "there is no doubt that Stonehenge was an ancient observatory". According to his observations the construction is not as old as earlier believed; it was done more likely between 1900 B.C. and 1600 B.C. The original great ditch that surrounds the Stonehenge was constructed around 1900 BC by Neolithic farmers. The standard measure was megalithic yard 2.72 feet. A miniature Stonehenge was discovered on a hilltop in Loch Rob in the Outer Hebrides in 1934. It was found that a long avenue running North-South pointed at the pole star. In fact it was a vast calculating arrangement designed to predict the eclipses of the moon. Stonehenge had sixty stones in its outer circle - thirty upright menhirs and thirty horizontal lintels as they were originally erected. The entire field of this structure was therefore related to the sixty-year cycle in astronomy as enunciated by of Hindus, Dagon and Chaldeans who believe that the sixty-year cycle is based on the astronomical event when the two farther planets, Jupiter and Saturn come together in close alignment once every sixty years. The Hindu sixty-year cycle is known as Brihaspati, the Hindu name for Jupiter.

The earth force consists of two currents, Yin and Yang, the negative and the positive. In this connection the Chinese concept of Feng-Shui is relevant. It is the 'art of adopting the residences of the living and the dead so as to cooperate and harmonise with the local currents of the cosmic breath. The force and nature of the invisible currents would vary from hour to hour since it is being constantly modified by the position of the heavenly bodies.' In 1974 Alexander Thomas put forward a theory that Stonehenge was an observatory to study the movements of the moon. The place was used for festivals and pagan rites. The latter were banned in 1985 to avoid vandalism.

MENHIRS AND DOLMENS

The word menhir is a combination of two words - 'men' means long, and 'hir' means stone. It was adopted from the French during 19th century. It is a very tall heavy standing upright monumental stone while dolmen are prehistoric megalithic tombs. Dolmen are based on a three tier structure --- two vertical short basalt megaliths topped by a horizontal one, thereby creating a well protected strong cavity to act as a tomb. Golan Heights used to be littered with hundreds of dolmens, but how many are still there in existence is a matter for verification.

Menhirs are found all over the globe as relics of prehistoric times. They are scattered all over Scandinavia, Sweden, France, Armenia, South America, Asia, Siberia, India, etc. Besides Great Britain, Ireland and Brittany they are generally more common in

Western Europe. One fallen and now broken menhir in Brittany measured over sixty feet while many stones in that region are between ten and twenty feet high. Indeed, it baffles the imagination how such extremely heavy unwieldy pieces could be erected in those primitive times. There are about 1,200 of them in France and were erected as part of the Megalithic Culture that flourished in Europe at those past distant times. In the Middle Ages the erect standing stones were seen to have been built by giants who inhabited the Planet in those times. This was before the biblical floods. However, many megaliths were destroyed or defaced by early Christians who considered these monuments evil and irreligious. At one time there were said to have been about 50,000 megaliths all over the globe but at present there are about 10,000 in various parts, including a substantial number in India. It is believed that the Druids used these megalithic stones for human sacrifice. Many megaliths were found to have been carved with megalithic art, albeit the motifs were not clear.

MEGALITHIC CULTURE IN INDIA

An archeological site in Mudumala in Mahbubnagar District of Andhra Pradesh was found dotted with about eighty big menhirs, some as tall as 14 feet, buried 4-7 feet deep underground indicating thereby the very heavy weight that was lifted up and positioned vertically via ancient crude mechanisms. In addition, numerous smaller ones were found scattered all over the agricultural fields. The site was investigated by Dr. K.V. Rao. His team discovered that particular rows of stones were aligned to the rising and setting sun on days of summer and winter solstice. By implication it means that the megalithic community was aware of the solar trajectories. The similarity and common features of the Andhra site with those of the Stone Henge megaliths of

Britain, and their cultural implications seem to have been missed by some scholars ...

I have personally seen and photographed one Single-Megalithic memorial in the remote interior of Khasi-Hills district in the erstwhile province of Assam, now Meghalaya. I was attracted to the site out of sheer curiosity while driving on Shillong-Jowai Road way back in early 1950's. This picture of a single menhir, placed below, was published in January 1956 issue of Vanyajati, a magazine devoted to social anthropology along with one of my articles. Much as I tried to obtain further information about this single tall stone, no one could throw any light on the subject.

The word 'megalith' has its origin in ancient Greek culture. It generally refers to a large stone structure or monument standing either alone by itself, or in a group with other similar monuments: megas meaning large and imposing, and lithos meaning stone. 'Megalithic' culture therefore represents a construction distinguished by presence of large size stones, dressed or naturally rough, used for funerary or other social ceremonies. The custom and the system of such constructions date back to ancient, possibly prehistoric times. There is a wide variety of such stone monuments all over India, both in the north, north-east as well as in Kerala and Andhra Pradesh in the south. However, here we are concerned with North-East India, particularly Khasi and Jaintia-Hills districts of Meghalaya. There are extensive large fields of such megaliths at Mawphlang near Shillong which I had personally visited during my posting at Shillong, besides Cherrapunjee, Jowai, et al. Such concentrations also exist in Nagaland and Manipur, besides a number of other places which are of ethno-archeological interest.

A solitary Monolithic Memorial astrideShillong-Jowai Road
In Jaintia Hills District of erstwhile Assam Province
Photo taken by the Author in early **1950's** with his Driver
Standing beside the Monument

The most common type of megalith found in Assam is menhir: a single dressed or undressed monument. The root of the word 'menhir' is French: men meaning stone and hir meaning long. It could be anything from 100 cm up to about 450 cm or so in length, standing alone, all by itself, as a monument to whatever, with its base driven into the ground. Nangbah village in Jaintia-Hills is well known for its large concentration of menhirs. Amongst the Khasi and Syntengs (Jaintias) the custom of erecting menhirs in alignments and avenues in honor of the dead is still practiced. They believe that it helps the living kith and kin. So it does amongst the Nagas of Nagaland. It is indeed astonishing that ancients could handle such heavy megaliths without any of the modern lifting-erecting contrivances. In short, the British Stonehenge and their French equivalents are not the only marvels of their type. Who copied whom? How did the two cultures, geographically so much distance apart come into close contact? Who copied whom? If anyone at all did copy!

Here it may be recalled that in 1975 in commemoration of centenary celebrations of State capital of Shillong in Meghalaya, the State Government arranged for a few megaliths to be brought all the way up the mountains. These were set up in the center of the city as memorial of the occasion. Just goes to show that modern educated elite too continue to follow the practice of erecting menhirs ...

On the other end of the spectrum are flat stones slabs resting on 3-4 smaller vertical supports. These are called Dolmens which, in Celtic means stone-table. These structures are seen in Khasi-Hills in front of a row of menhirs, usually the tallest one. Incidentally, amongst the Khasi the tallest menhir is an honor reserved for the eldest maternal uncle as a symbolic gesture of their matrilineal society, while the youngest daughter known as 'khadduh' inherits the family home and property[1].

Christopher von FÜRER-HAIMENDORF, an anthropologist of repute, during his visit to the Miri Hills of North East India, witnessed a ceremony in which a vertical stone was erected in honor of the village Chief, another in honor of the European visitor, and a third one in horizontal position in honor of his wife. This was a symbolic pact of friendship between the plainsmen and hill tribes of the area, with a promise that no harm would ever come to any visitors from the Government side.[2]

References

1. "Gemini Paul" (The Author's pseudonym): The Place of Khadduh — the youngest Daughter in Khasi and Syntengs Society; Vanyajati, Vol. 4 April 1956, No. 2
2. Christoph Haimendorf: Himalayan Barbarity; John Murray, London 1955; p. 218

4

Bermuda Triangle

The mysterious area in the Atlantic Ocean, bounded by Florida, Bermuda and Puerto Rico, is notorious for paranormal events of a tragic nature. It is also called the Devil's Triangle, Twilight Zone, Port of Missing Ships, etc. It is one of the most mysterious and dangerous areas of the earth's oceans. Over 2000 vessels and 75 airplanes have vanished in this stretch of water over the past three centuries. And that too without any apparent cause either! One of the vessels carried a few hundred tons of gold stolen from the natives of North American continent. Was it divine retribution? Where have they all disappeared? How and why? Why can't modern science and technology search them out? There is no answer to these riddles although in rare cases ships have been found but not a single passenger or crew member.

Ever since the famed explorer Christopher Columbus sailed through the area during his epic voyage to America, strange phenomena have been reported from that stretch of water. Columbus had noted in his logs in October 1492 that the compass behaved erratically, crew had seen "strange dancing lights on the horizon", "Flames in the sky", and that a strange unexplained light emanated from the sea. That is the first known documentation of strange anomalies of a small oceanic area, East of Gulf of Mexico, spread over between Miami, San Juan-Bermuda in the Atlantic Ocean.

December 05, 1905 was a nice sunny calm day, with ideal flying conditions. But six Navy planes and their crew just vanished, as if in thin air. That is when the area was named as the Bermuda Triangle. Before that a number of ships had suffered a similar fate. Other phenomena witnessed from the area include bright lights and balls of fire, sudden red flares that appear to be explosions turning the sky yellow, hazy and foggy. Air crews have reported sudden power failures, compass-spinning, strong magnetic pulls towards the water below and their inability to control the altitude.

The most notable event which finally occurred on December15, 1945 when Flight 19 comprising of five Scavenger Torpedo Bombers lifted off the Naval Air Station at Fort Lauderdale. It was a practice run for 13 student-pilots under Lieutenant Charles Taylor. As they passed over the mysterious waters the compass behaved erratically. The plain lost its course and the pilot his sense of direction. Soon it was flying to nowhere, ran short of fuel and dropped into the ocean killing all crew members. A PBM Marine plane with 13 crew members went out in search of the missing bomber and that too vanished without a trace. Was it the unlucky number 13!

Do the spirits from the Other-Side residing in the area of the Triangle have some secret to hide from the living humans? No wonder the fishermen believe that devils, demons and monsters inhabit the danger zone. And that they kidnap the ships. Some hold hidden sea beings responsible for the losses while others point accusing finger to the good old Atlantis whose disappearance under the sea remains an unsolved catastrophic mystery, if at all there was an island-continent like that. Under sea volcanic activity has been blamed by others.

PSYCHIC CURES and CURSES

Besides the foregoing geographically oriented instances of hidden powers, may be supernatural as believed by some, there are numerous historical examples of psychic cures and surgeries. These are galore in Tibetan and other Eastern literature as part of the prevailing folklore. The first that comes to mind is from Brazil where one Dr. Eirigo is known to have some gifted talent and acumen. He used the vital energies of the body in conjunction with spiritual healing. The former is of course an important part of Indian Yogic system of treatment.

The ancient civilisation of Egypt too had its 'prescriptions' for psychic cures. The rock-inscriptions of Egypt are a living testimony of that talent. Some inscriptions depict 'doctors' with one hand kept on the patient's stomach and the other on his back. Christian faithful strongly believe that Saint Bernard miraculously bestowed eye sight to ten blind persons besides curing about a dozen physically handicapped persons in a single day using his elevated spiritual powers. Saint Patrick is believed to have restored eye sight to a blind man by merely blessing him with his hands on his eyes. Tibetan doctors have carried out surgical procedures without any anesthesia and suturing the wound by merely caressing the affected area with the palms of their hands ... It is all a matter of faith and belief.

Another story on the same lines pertains to a villager near Kentucky in USA. Edgar Keisei was inflicted with severe rheumatic pain and spasms. Some doctors attending on the patient suddenly realised that, although otherwise unconscious, all of a sudden he was sitting upright and talking some gibberish some of which included names of some medicines which the doctors could recognise. No one in the village had ever learnt any Latin nor was conversant with the Latin terminology for the diseases, or their treatment. His unexpected arousal from an exceptional state of unconsciousness leading to activation of hidden layers of some extra-sensory powers enabled him to diagnose and cure dreaded disease in different parts of the world. Indeed, truth is stranger than fiction

More on this subject later in this work ...

Charles Berlitz: *The Bermuda Triangle*; New York, 1974

5

Shamanism and Shamanic Experiences

There are numerous verified and recorded instances of trance-channel communication. One of the best pertains to the sinking of the mail-steamer The Pacific. Emma Floyd Britten (1823-1899) had travelled on this ship across the Atlantic Ocean to New York. During the voyage she and her mother had come to know a number of crew members one of whom was Mr. Smith. The spirit of Smith appeared before Emma and told her that the ship had sunk and he was dead; so were all other crew and passengers. Emma informed the owners of the vessel who threatened to sue her for spreading false rumors. However, it soon transpired that information channeled to Emma by the spirit of Smith was correct and that the Pacific had indeed been lost to the sea. Casualties in high altitude mountain climbing, over the oceans, accidents and earthquakes, tsunami, etc. are the usual circumstances channeling information by the spirits through some receptive mediums. Spirit communication is not the same thing as telepathy, nor is it comparable to reading the omens. However, it does reinforce the concept that "our near and dear ones on 'the other side' are watching over us."

Following her divorce Lynn V. Andrews saw an intriguing Native American basket in Los Angeles in a photography exhibition. May be she did not see any such thing in a photo but thought she did. She was obsessed by the image and travelled to Manitoba in Canada where she painstakingly tracked down the basket to Agnes Whistling Elk, a Cree medicine woman. Andrews met the Agnes and her blind colleague, Ruby Plenty Chiefs. However, there were no means she could have managed to make contact with the woman who knew about the mysterious basket — a sacred marriage basket that could not be purchased but had to be won. At that time the basket was in possession of a white man named, Red Dog, turned sorcerer while under apprenticeship of Agnes whistling Elk. He wanted to acquire all the female power for himself and had stolen the basket from Agnes.

Andrews was not prepared to give up. So she joined Agnes as an apprentice. Agnes told Andrews that she would have to be a bridge between the tribal and industrial cultures, and to write a book on her experiences. Thus Andrews became the first white woman to join the sisterhood of the Shields, a secret society of forty-four Shaman women from various tribal cultures. The Society had dedicated itself towards preserving their shamanic cultural tradition. Soon Andrews managed to retrieve the basket from Red Dog and got into other shamanistic initiations. Andrews has authored four adventurous and two other books drawing on her long experience of close association with tribal communities. However, the Native Americans felt that they had been misrepresented while she insisted that she was merely trying to reinstate the feminine consciousness.

6

Divination

Divination is the art of foretelling the future, of obtaining knowledge of the unknown -- using omens, visions, portents and other (secret) divinatory tools. It is a gift from the divine, from the gods; and hence the term divination. At its very lowest level of intelligence, most gypsies are expert in divination in one form or the other; such as card-reading, palm-reading, casting runes or dice, crystal gazing, etc.

At the other end of the spectrum is Trance, divination in another form, and has been a route to high level policy decision-making, a common feature of Tibetan state-craft. His Highness the Dalai Lama while in Lhasa, and even while at Dharmsala in India often convened, and still does, a meeting of high dignitaries for consultations where the State Oracle (The Nechung Oracle) goes into trance and answers question of high level state policy. The ancient Chinese, the Babylonians, the Chaldeans, Egyptians - all had their well paid priests, dreaming all the time as to what the future had in store for their lords. Similarly, the oracles of ancient Greece were reputed in divinations and prophecies. The Oracles of Delphi, Epidaurus and Trophonius were well known. Some oracles used to accompany the armed forces going into battle so that they could forewarn and advise them.

In this connection we may recall the experience of Abraham Lincoln when he and his wife were given a lecture-cum-advice at a séance by a young girl who had gone into spontaneous trance. She spoke at length for almost an hour about the desirability of immediate emancipation of the slaves. A similar scene was repeated at yet another séance where the President and his Lady Wife were present and were lectured by the young girl about the necessity of immediate emancipation. Freedom for the slaves was a hot topic of the day for the administration and the public at large. Not only that, this young girl also advised the President of the United States of America to visit the army camps to boost morale of the troops. The President was thus convinced of the course of action he should follow, more so since the command for that line of action had come from the angel world through the ever watchful all-seeing Spirit.

Divination was done both for an individual, for a group, or for the royalty and the State. In its simplest form it could well be done by judging a flight of birds! Right or wrong is immaterial. Divining rod used to be a common tool for locating water and minerals. Professional water-diviners were in vogue too. It was all a matter of psychic skill.

The appearance of "flying saucers", UFOs (Unidentified Flying Objects), the Bermuda Triangle, the lost continent Atlantis, etc. have given a new twist to the power of Spirits. The sightings of nine shining traveling against the background of Mount Ranger in Washington State on June 24, 1947 added to the speculation that homo-sapiens and their gods all came from outer space, some other planetary system to help man colonise the planet earth. The ensuing debate about the veracity of scientific theory of evolution revived the age old controversial belief that our ancestors came from outer space some fifty thousand years ago when the homo-sapiens had not been fully evolved. The idea of race of small-statured people inhabiting Planet Earth added yet another complication. Kidnapping of human beings by the aliens have also been recorded/reported. But it is virtually impossible to be categorical on such matters connected with the 'spirit world', or extra-terrestrial civilisations. However, one can say with confidence that out of millions of galaxies, planet earth could not possibly be the only spot in this immense Universe to support like an intelligence system resembling what we have on this Planet. In fact it is well on the cards the extra-terrestrial intelligence could be more advanced and better developed than ours. The logical conclusion was that massive structures like pyramids could not possibly have been built by the pygmy inhabitants of Planet Earth; the great pyramids were the fruits of labor of the giants from outer space. *2001: A Space Odyssey, a 1968-film by Stanley Kubrick* "transformed the idea into intellectual mythology of the twentieth century." The next phase of this transformation was that the pyramids, as huge as they were, could not possibly have been built by men of those times and were therefore built by spacemen.

Spirits do play 'games' with us in the mortal world. Strange things happen in haunted houses. The spirit(s) occupying the house may indulge in knockings and rapping which can be quite scary for the occupants of the house. However, if the people in the house have the patience and are not afraid, they can communicate with the spirit by asking questions and receiving answers in the manner requested. Belief in spiritualism is a pre-requisite for communicating with the spirit world. If a person has been murdered in a house, his spirit may continue to remain in the house and provide information about the events leading to the murder and details about the accused person(s).

A newly married completely sober man from Devonshire moved into a coastal cottage. Two weeks after the honeymoon he returned home completely drunk. This episode was repeated a second time after a couple of weeks. The young wife consulted a 'wise woman' who pointing to a wooden armchair in the room and advised the young lady to burn that chair. She complied. There was no trouble after that. Further investigation revealed that chair belonged to a drunken butcher who had committed suicide while sitting on it. In another case of a haunted house: a rat, a cat, a dog and a rattlesnake were taken to a house in Kentucky where in two of the known haunted rooms two violent deaths had taken place. The dog snarled and backed out of one of the rooms; no amount of cajoling would make it change its mind to obey the commands of its master. The cat was carried into room in the lap of the owner. No sooner they crossed the threshold the cat leapt over the shoulder and dug in its claws for safety. However while the rat merely sniffed around the place, the rattlesnake immediately adopted the attack posture towards the empty chair in the room. None of the creatures showed any reaction when they were taken to other rooms where the tragedy had not taken place. It was not the entire house that was haunted; only the specific rooms of the house were indeed haunted. This case was investigated by Dr. Robert Morris, a psychologist affiliated with the psychical foundation of Durham, North Carolina. Edward Russell calls these imprints on the structures as recordings of "T-Fields" (Thought-Fields) of horror or despair. 'These powerful thoughts of violence, horror and murder get saturated in the building material of the structure to last indefinitely.'

It is well known that in the past the Western philosophy did not accept the Eastern versions of occult practices, spiritualism, after-life, ghosts and haunted houses, etc. This mental block has now given way to open acceptance of OBE, NDE, Astral Projection, etc. In so far as the Americans are concerned they have readily accepted these occult practices as part and parcel of life. For instance: A Gallup Poll held in 1980 revealed that 71 per cent of Americans believe in Life after Death while a similar Poll held in 2001 showed that 38 per cent of them believe that it is possible to make contact with the dead. Going a step further, 42 per cent of Americans believe in ghosts and haunting. Ghosts may be there and a place may be haunted but it is not necessary that everyone who visits the place would see a ghost. That indeed is the characteristic of ghosts and haunting. Most Britons believe that UFOs do exist. In fact, nine per cent of them insist that they have seen a UFO one time or the other while 43 per cent of them believe in alien life. After all, UFOs do land and take off vertically as our spacecraft do. The analogy is perfectly logical and rational.

One night in 1965 Ted Owen, age forty-five, was driving along a road with his daughter near Fort Worth, Texas. Suddenly, he and his daughter saw a great cigar shaped object flashing colored lights, approaching over the next field. As it came near the car, suddenly all lights turned off and the object vanished in thin air. They suspected that they had actually seen a UFO. Other experiences with UFOs are indeed equally odd. Films and tape recordings of UFOs turn out to be blank. Police radios which are switched off sudden crackle with loud unintelligible messages. Calls come through on disconnected telephone lines. Cows and sheep are found with their necks neatly slit and their bodies drained of blood. Pet dogs and cats disappear in large numbers. Some Westerners have come to believe that UFOs are controlled by beings from other worlds who do not wish to let the humanity into their secrets, for whatever reasons. My be all this hocus-pocus is in fact mere paranormal activity, and no more! We just cannot draw a line between the latent powers of the human mind, and the invisible powers that may exist around us in the universe. The episode of a Satsang at Dakshineshwar in the Ashram of Swami Ramakrishna is a classic example of infinite hidden powers of the human mind. A stranger entered the hall where hundreds of disciples and devotees had gathered for darshan of the Swami who had never met or seen this stranger. But he started scolding this man like a mother would do to her mischievous child. He said to the stranger: "You have beaten your wife at home and have come here for devotion? Go back! First beg her pardon and then come here for Satsang." The stranger was shocked; he confessed and went back home. The audience was stunned. Swamiji humbly explained to them: Human mind has infinite power. It can reach anywhere in the world and even acquire hidden information in a fraction of moments, provided of course its power is not drained abruptly in pernicious passions and haphazard activities. No doubt human mind is the most evolved manifestation of the supreme consciousness in Nature, a repository of sentimental and spiritual powers hidden in his inner self that reflect his divine realms of eternal consciousness.

One day when Nobel Laureate, Mr. Richard Bach was taking a stroll on a beach he heard a strange voice calling him repeatedly by the name of "Jonathan Livingstone Seagull". Richard did not know any one by that name nor had anyone had ever called him by that name. And there was not a soul around the place; He was absolutely alone, all by himself. He was dazed, as if hypnotised and started writing furiously. Amazingly, he completed a novel of 400 pages within the hours of that night with absolutely no background of writing fiction, not even a short story or poem, all his previous life. It was an extraordinary case of psychic powers of ESP (Extra Sensory Perception).

The studies on PSI and ESP, the supernatural powers of human self have opened up the channels for deeper and wider and scientific research on other disciplines of spirituality too thereby rediscovering the ancient wisdom of divine era of spiritual enlightenment of mankind. (Quoted by Pandit Shriram Sharma Acharya; p. 152)

Another episode to illustrate the same point from a different perspective: A tantric was extremely jealous of spiritual accomplishments of Guru Gorakhnath. So he decided to kill this great yogi. Once they encountered each other in a forest. The tantric had an axe in his hand. He ran towards the yogi but some invisible force halted him in his steps, about ten feet from the Guru, with his right hand holding the axe in the air and left hand held back on his back as if tied down, unable to make any movement. He stood still like a stone while the Guru stood still in front of him, calmly smiling. His disciples were wonder struck. The Guru explained to them: Controlled and enlightened mind is like an obedient giant endowed with supernatural powers. You merely had a glimpse of its enormous miraculous capabilities ... And that is what happened when Brahmchari Vyasdeva, looking famished and hungry, met a sage in a mountain cave. When asked what he would like to eat to quench his hunger, he blurted out '*jalebis*', the warm sweets famous for their taste and fragrance in North India. The sage went inside the cave and brought out a plateful of warm sweet *jalebis*. But when Vyasdeva went inside the cave, he saw nothing, no utensils, no materials and no fire. The sage laughed and explained: Human mind is a repository of supernatural powers. Once it is refined, spiritually activated and trained by yoga-sâdhnâs, it can extract anything from anywhere in the world, and transform it into any desired form without any constraint of time ... Swami Vivekananda cites a similar experience with a Brahmin tantric, having occult powers, while on a tour of Hyderabad region. However, when the Swamiji visited the Tantric his son was suffering from high fever, and was told that he could not perform for the visitors since his mind was distracted by serious illness of his son. Nevertheless, if the great Swami blessed his son by putting his on his head, the boy would become alright and he could then show his magical capabilities to Swamiji. When all was done the tantric took a simple blanket like any other lying around the place. The visitors made a thorough check of the blanket to make sure it was indeed empty with no hidden pockets or any such extraneous items. He wrapped the blanket around his body. He would put his hands inside the blanket and produced all sorts of eats, refreshments, Whatever the visitors asked for, he would just put his hands inside the blanket, close his eyes and produce the desired item, so much so at one point of time he produced a huge bunch of red roses, glistening with fresh dew — These experiences demonstrate that the supernormal attainments of *Siddhis* like *Animâ, Garimâ, Laghimâ, Prâkamp, Istwa,* et al, are not mere figs of imagination. They do have a scientific basis which recent discoveries, technological developments and researches are in the process of proving them to be so.[1]

LASER (Light Amplification of Simulated Emission of Radiation) is the latest tool in the grasp of scientists, surgeons, medical technicians, besides the military of course who have now developed the power to destroy a target at about 1,86,000 miles in less than a second. LASER could replace television and empower us to witness real events live, thereby crediting Sanjay's story in Mahabharata War that he witnessed via supernormal vision of his mental eye. In the process telepathy may also get credence!

According to Hindu mysticism, the Rod of Brahma has three channels: the central channel is called Sushumma. It is generally blocked by the head of the serpent. The left channel Ida is female in character while the right channel, Pingala, is male in its essence. The Kundalini energy somehow found its way through the male channel Pingala which was already red hot solar and fiery in character. When Gopi Krishna suffered excruciating pains in his head, he managed to summon the lunar energy Ida which cascaded down his spinal cord bathing the entire body with cool soothing peace and calm.

The foregoing statistics-episodes just show a major transformation in mental make-up of Western minds during the past half century. Tibetan Diaspora that ushered in concepts of Buddhism, and the lecture tours of His Holiness the Dalai Lama, have further strengthened the transformation of Western mind-set.

Divination is the art of finding the lost, identifying the guilty, foretelling the future at individual or collective level, thereby serving an important social function by resolving disputes and providing a means for solving problems. The priests, prophets, oracles, shamans, witch-doctors, medicine-man, psychic and such other persons reputed to possess supernatural powers are customarily responsible for 'divination'. Skilled diviners possess a keen sense of intuition and an innate understanding of human psychology. After all, it is their bread and butter!

Divination is more common in the East than in Western societies. Consulting horoscopes of marriageable children is common pre-marital proceedings between the two families. It would not be wrong to say that in India is an accepted way of daily life amongst folks. On the other hand Christianity in the West had, and continues to, forbid divinations calling it witchcraft. Nevertheless, divination has never been completely eradicated from the Western world despite religious prohibitions. An average person has an overpowering desire to know about his personal future than to worry about religious dogmas on the subject.

Cultures the world over have devised innumerable techniques for divination, which fall in two broad categories:

- Interpretation of natural or artificial signs, omens, portents and lots;
- Direct communication with gods and spirits via visions, trance, dreams and possessions.

All divination is an attempt to reach the supernatural to ascertain the will of the god(s). Even in respect of lots and interpretation of signs itis assumed that the will of god is reflected. A typical divination consists of advice as well as prediction, generally more of the former than the latter.

In ancient times divination used to be a royal privilege. The process was used to decide state-level policy matters, matters of war and peace, forecast natural disasters thereby mitigate their ill effects, and so on. The royalty employed state-level diviners whose very jobs or lives were dependent upon accuracy of their divination skills. The ancient Chinese had court astrologers, and so have the present Tibetans too. The early Egyptian priests slept in temples so that they could dream the future through kind courtesy of the gods. I wonder if they still do so in mosques!

The Chaldeans and Babylonians had elaborate divinatory systems under the priests. The ancient Romans too did the same. They had a special caste of diviner-priests called 'augurs' who claimed to have the ability to interpret such natural phenomena as flight of birds, cloud formations, smoke etc. Amongst the tribal societies the world over, particularly in India, the entrails of slaughtered sacrificial animals were carefully examined. The liver rather than the heart was considered as the central organ for divination purposes. The Greeks followed almost the same system as the present day Tibetans in as much as they divined dreams and consulted special oracles that went into trance to allow the gods to speak through them as the medium. The most famous Greek Oracle resided at Delphi, near the base of Mount Parnassus. Astrological horoscope was their specialty. In Indian tribal societies divination is not necessarily a function of the Chief of the village or clan. Any villager who has a problem and the means may resort to divination by the village priest. Shamans perform this function in Shamanistic societies. They go into trance to communicate with spirit-helpers. In Africa the King's Diviner is backed by the force of law. They generally use one or more of the following techniques:-

- Place two sticks in the anthill and see which stick has been eaten by the following day;
- Board Rubbing: Two pieced of wood are rubbed and yield an answer when they stick together;
- Benge Oracle: Benge poison obtained from a plant similar to strychnine is fed to chicken. The length and nature of the fowl's death throes provide the answer. And if the fowl survives, that too is an answer.

In Western Uganda the Labara tribesmen fill small pots with medicines, which represent the suspects of the crime. The pots are set on fire. Whichever pot does not boil over is a pointer towards the guilty one. In another method the suspects are made to drink an awful potion or stew; the guilty one will suffer indigestion. Sortilege, the casting of stones or bones or shells, is another technique common to many tribal societies. The pattern of their fall reveals an answer. In recent times use of 'divining rod', a pendulum in conjunction with the theory that every object has a field that extends around it. Its radius is the 'rate' for that object. "So, for example, a copper penny would have a field exactly thirty and a half inches wide, extending around it, as well as upward and downward in the form of a cone."[2] This 'field theory' modifies the 'cryptesthesia' theory because the in many cases of dowsing the diviner has actually been able to see the underground water. It is therefore well on the cards that emotions can impress themselves on any kind of fields while water has a peculiar kind of field. Dowsers believe that sleeping above an underground stream is the cause of much illness. May be, long-term exposure to the radiation of water could be as harmful as that to radio-activity.

References

1. Pandit Shriram Acharya: op. cit. pp.117-119
2. Colin Wilson: MYSTERIES; Watkins Publishing, London, 2006; p. 61

7

Precognition, Premonitions, Predictions and Prophecies

Precognition means "to know before-hand". It is paranormal knowledge of future events, that something specific is going to happen. It falls in the field of Extra Sensory Perception (ESP) in which perception of the future is obtained via extraordinary means. Jean Dixon's precognition of assassination of John F. Kennedy is a classic example of this faculty coming into action. Yet another equally classic example is that of a 34-year old marine engineer who refused three times in a row to sign on as the second engineer for the maiden voyage of the most luxurious and expensive passenger ship, the famous TITANIC. He had a gut-feeling that something terrible was going to happen!

Premonition is a form of foreboding or forewarning of possible future accidents, disasters, death etc. The first one is generally positive albeit about 25 per cent could be negative, the last one mostly negative while predictions and prophecies could be either. ESP is no longer merely speculative. Recent scientific tests have proved that man possesses faculties beyond in addition to the five normal physical senses, thereby confirming the occultists' claim that 'truth is universal, omnipresent existence of nature which gradually becomes discovered and proven and realised faculty' ... Para-psychology thus compels physical materialism to don the uniform of metaphysics.[1] Neila Jones of South London who came to be popularly known as "Alien Spy" is an interesting fascinating example of clairvoyance at its best. She had no connection with the Scotland Yard or London Police but possessed an uncanny power of resolving many mysterious knotty cases left beyond unresolved by the intelligence department. She would just around in her house and focus her mind at the specific case and get to the 'missing link' and secret information through the powers of her clairvoyance abilities. Thus she served the London Police for more than fifteen years. Some subjects have fingertips so sensitive that they can read an entire newspaper with their Herbert B. Greenhouse: Premonition, A Leap into the Future; New York, 1971

Dr. J.B. Rhine of Duke University at Durham (USA) is considered as a pioneer in the new field of Parapsychology.

These are instances of "sixth sense" on which enormous research has been done to verify the facts. Indeed, the human body and mind have immense reservoirs of just waiting to be tapped by the right person (s) at the right time. However, it should be borne in mind that these immense potentials are all within us; nothing comes from outside the human mind. Thus Mind is a special kind of 'matter', light or other forms of energy. Whatever it is, the 'third eye' or the sixth sense activated in the human mind endows it with supernatural potentials of a special kind.

A 1958-episode from Philadelphia illustrates the point more pointedly - Hegel Lambert was returning home from her office in Pensbury Whites. After dropping a colleague at Delmar Avenue she decided to turn towards a nearby market to run some errands. After driving for a few kilometers she had an inner feeling that she had made a grave mistake. She reversed her car and started driving in the opposite direction from her home and before she knew whether she was coming or going home, she was ahead of the Hill Street Crossing. And the sight she saw made her shiver in fear: A two year old boy was hanging on the slab of snow above the icy canal flowing beside the hills. She took her car near the horrified boy but before she could commence her rescue efforts, her car was down a snow-ditch and she just could not open the doors to get out. Constant beeping of the horn attracted the attention of George Taylor and his 14-years old son. They both came over and recued the small boy and also managed to get Hegel's car back on the road. This is a true story of 'Precognition', an inner voice inspiring the person to follow a certain line of action.

Premonition is an experience somewhat akin to precognition --- It was March 1951. Forty years old Charles Bogoratz, a police officer in Los Angeles, and his wife were browsing through some insurance documents when all of a sudden Charles blurted out to his wife: "Merlin, I don't know why I am feeling that soon I will encounter a mishap. Something might happen to me. In that case please do not get loose your courage and patience." And then they went off to sleep. A few days after this conversation, Charles was called to arrest two hoodlums in Washington Boulevard on the west coast. They were looting shops at gun point but tried to run away after they saw the police. One of the robbers shot in panic and bullet went straight through Charles's skull; he died at the spot. Unfortunately, his premonition had materialised!

Instant premonition is an aspect of usual premonition. Two interesting cases have been reported in California press (where I lived for some years). The first is from Modesto where Paul Stuart, while engrossed in her office work, suddenly felt that some tragedy had taken place back home. She called her father and asked him to go over to her house to see if all was well. When the old man was on his way to the house, he found his grandson, while riding his bike, had slipped into a side-ditch and the pistol he was holding in his hand accidently fired straight into his chest killing him at the spot.

The second episode of instant premonition also comes from California. Clifford Mac had invited his business partner Abraham Isere for business-lunch meeting. Both wives were also present at the table. After some time, Isere suddenly felt that Mac's wife was in some serious trouble. He screamed involuntarily and insisted that Mac break open the bathroom door. Mac was flabbergasted at this request and was very reluctant to comply. However, when Isere was about to call police for help, Mac agreed and both tried to break open the door. Mac called his wife twice, but no response. When they finally managed to break open the door, they saw Mac's wife lying unconscious with her head in the water in the bath-tub. She was rushed to Emergency and put through 3 days of intensive care to recover and return home.

The foregoing incidents lead us to believe that "if our mind could grasp some subliminal signals so naturally in ordinary case, then what if we attempt training it and try arousing its hidden potentials?"

Predictions fall in the sphere of Prophecy in which psychic ability plays a vital role to obtain information about future events. Similarly, the difference between precognition and premonition is rather blurry. The former pertains to some specific event while the later is generally a vague sense or feeling that some unknown event is likely to take place. Almost all the above mentioned characteristics have been known in operation since ancient times. All prophecy is precognition but all precognition is not prophecy which has an element of divine inspiration.

Precognition generally comes via dreams and is the most common form of ESP, about 60 per cent to 70 per cent. Here the dreamer "perceives" an event in the future that later turns out to be true. Vast majority of experiences in this category pertain to death, dying or other negative experiences. To quote one true instance: In the Welsh village of Aberfan, a nineyear old girl had a dream on the night of October 20, 1966 that there was no school the following day. She did not dream that there would be no classes; instead, she actually dreamt there was no school. The next morning she told her mother that something black came all over the school. But she went to school all the same. Shortly after nine that morning a half million ton of coal waste, saturated by days of incessant rains, slid down over the village buying houses and the entire school. Yes, there was really no school in Aberfan that morning! In the same vein, an Eightyyearold Quaker, John H. Williams, woke up at 8:55 a.m. on May 31, 1933 with vivid memory of a dream in which he heard the radio commentary on the Derby horse race to be run at 2:00 p.m. that afternoon. Williams was no punter but just out of sheer curiosity he heard the commentary of that race and was astonished that all details including the names of horses and the order in which they ran tallied exactly with what he had dreamt the night before.

Can you believe that effects can precede causes? Yes, they can, contrary to basic laws of science and common sense! A team of British scientists ran a series of closely controlled and very complex tests on British psychic Malcolm Besant, at the Maimonides Medical Center. The tests conclusively proved that effects can precede causes.[2]

However, dreams are not the only medium of ESP. It may occur spontaneously in waking visions, auditory hallucinations besides thoughts that suddenly flash into the mind; it is a sense of knowing. As in all such psychic activities, precognition may also occur via trance, channeling, mediums and divination. Generally speaking, this type of ESP occurs within 24-48 hours of the event. Severe emotional shock plays an important role in precognition which could also take place, rather rarely, even much later than the 24-48 hour time span. Intimacy with the subject is a key factor, e.g. family members, spouse, close friends etc. Casual acquaintances come into the picture only in cases of disasters, plane crashes and earthquakes. Precognition seems to demonstrate that in some baffling cases the future events have already taken place; the effects precede the causes! Sounds absurd and illogical, but precisely what paranormal phenomenon brings to light. We have reached a stage in our mental development when paranormal is expected to cover such subjects as psychic surgery, transcendental meditation, bio-feedback, multiple personality, UFO's, plant telepathy, et al. Some of my stories have covered some of these subjects, albeit not in depth.

Seeking access to the future has been part of human psyche since ancient times. The prophets and oracles have ruled the world over ages past. The Hindus and Greeks considered the future as immutable. Of late, the free will is accepted to change the perceived future. Nonetheless, it is estimated that precognition arising out of psychic research has proved useful in averting disasters in 30 per cent to 50 per cent cases. That is why it is accepted that precognition is more a glimpse than a definite unalterable forecast of an impending event --- good, bad or indifferent. However, another theory contends that the precognitive experience releases a powerful self-fulfilling psychokinetic energy which somehow contributes to one's own demise because of "scared to death" syndrome. Whatever be the contradictions in understanding precognition, it is one of the ESP experiences most susceptible to laboratory testing. It is generally not realised that precognitive experiences, the dreams, are most common, so common that most people do not recall the details or significance of their dreams.

Nevertheless, one peculiarity of precognition process is that one never forecasts one's own death. One notable exception is that of President Abraham Lincoln who dreamt of his own death six weeks prior to his assassination; but the dream was not of a violent death but of being an observer of after-event proceedings. Incidentally, America Presidents John Garfield and William McKinley also experienced foreknowledge of their violent deaths. "Living beings are endowed with the power of consciousness that is independent of the sense of organs and that can express its functions without the bodily sensors. What cannot be seen by the eyes, or heard by the ears, for instance, can be 'seen' or 'heard' through ESP." - Dr. I.S. Vekatschmily, Georgia Science University.

Following story illustrates the point: Russian Dog Tswala was extremely loyal and devoted to his master and protection of his property. He used to take the cattle for grazing all by himself, would know beforehand the route by which the attackers would be coming and change his track accordingly. One day a friend of his master required his services a few hundred miles away but he would not go willingly. So the Dog was put in a closed van and sent there. But he would neither drink water nor eat food and kept crying the whole day. Next day he just fled. Having been sent in a closed van, he had not even seen the route back home; but reached Tbilisi to his master. Dr. Vekatschmily heard the story, investigated the case, and carried out certain experiments. His conclusion: Some animals do possess an extra sensory 'eye' that helps them to work even without their biological eyes. Similar story about a Russian cat named Lyubes: She was supplied regular food at fixed hours kept in a fixed corner of a room. The experiment began with food being kept in a different room in a different corner; cat's eyes were closed tight with a strip of black cloth, and she left to fend for herself. Soon she reached the food platter. Next a set of stones were placed in lieu of food. She just did not bother! Cats do not have as strong a sense of smell as dogs, but they do learn pretty fast.

In November 1974 Dr. David M. Steward made an unusual announcement on California radio that based on supernatural signals received by his mind, on the 4th Thursday of this month when the California coast would be shaken by a severe tremor, but without any casualties. That is precisely what actually happened on 28th November of that year, a Thursday indeed.

An American reader writing in a Denver magazine in 1976 claimed that in August 1977 San Francisco and Pacific West Coast would experience a tremor of high seismic intensity. Till now no instrument has yet been invented that can predict an earthquake one year in advance. People ignored this prediction. But the devastating earthquake on August 13, 1977 did prove the veracity of the claim.

Unusual behaviour by birds and animals days before an earthquake strikes has been particularly noted from all over the globe, more so from the East. Rats and snakes feel the earth-vibrations well before the event and leave their holes before the calamity. Pigeons are known to fly away from their nests in the evening before the calamity. Rats and snakes feel the earth-vibrations much before the event and leave their holes for safety. Rabbits keep jumping restlessly with straightened ears.

Prediction is individualistic while prophecy is of collective nature on a grand scale dealing with national or groups-level. Nevertheless, prediction is just a form of prophecy. It is essentially based on precognition knowledge of which is may be obtained by through intuition, dreams, visions, astrological signs, Tarot, palmistry, numerology, and such other methods of divination. In shamanistic and oracular cultures drugs may be used to induce prophecy from a divine or supernatural force.

Premonitions generally tend to occur as forebodings of tragic events like death, accidents, disasters and similar other emotionally charged events. These are prophecies with a sense of foreboding and are generally sense-oriented, as opposed to precognitions which are precision-oriented. To cite a case in point: In 1948 Wolf Messing, a prominent Soviet psychic, was scheduled to perform in Ashkhabad. While walking through the streets he had a sudden terrible dread and an intense desire to get out soonest possible. For the first time in his life he cancelled all engagements in the town and left the City. Three days later a massive earthquake hit Ashkhabad killing 50,000 people. Of course the psychic had no forewarning of an impending earthquake-disaster.

The tragedy at Aberfan in Wales (October 21, 1966) killing 21 adults and 116 children in a rain soaked coal-waste slide, despite about 200 persons having had premonitions of impending disaster at least two weeks before the tragic event, has already been mentioned in this work. Premonitions are an intuitive early warning system that generally works during waking hours, and sometimes during repeated dreams state. To cite another instance: In the 1960's W.E. Cox examined rail passenger loads on American trains that were involved in accidents between 1950 and 1955. He compared the passenger loads on the same runs on the day of the accident, each of the preceding 7 days, 14 days and 28 days. He discovered a remarkable successive drop off in passenger counts. The Chicago and East-Illinois, Georgian, was carrying only nine passengers on the day of the accident on June 15, 1952, while just five days before it had carried the usual compliment of 62 passengers. Obviously many passengers had unconsciously altered their travel plans, or missed the train!

The same factor may prevent many people from sailing on doomed ships or aircraft. To cite another instance; The Titanic carried only 58 per cent of its passenger load on its disastrous maiden voyage in April 1912 in which 1,502 of the 2,207 passengers perished. The ship sank after collision with an iceberg. A lucky stroke of subconscious perhaps saved the lives of the 22 stokers who reported late for duty. Subsequent enquiries established that in seventeen cases intending passengers spread over England, America Canada and Brazil cancelled their passage during the two weeks prior to sailing date of the Titanic. Some of them dreamt that the ship was doomed while others felt uneasy going on a maiden voyage. In another case in the same vein, when the Empress of Ireland sank in River Lawrence in 1914 its first-class was two-thirds empty and second-class half-empty.

Yet another interesting incident of premonition was reported from a concert with a celebrated cellist. The producer of the programmers, Anne Own had a premonition that the cellist would break a string and asked the management what they would do if he did break a string. It was dismissed as an unlikely. However, a string did break eight minutes before end of the programme - premonition, or mere coincidence? Apparently, the former! These are small matters - like why a mirror reverses your left and right sides but not your head and feet! The mind has a tendency to bypass such trivial matters and concentrate on bigger issues.

Prophecy is divine inspired revelation of great events, of such great magnitude that that may affect entire countries. Here is a true story to prove the point -Edward Pearson was caught travelling without ticket in a London bound train on a chilly night of December 08, 1978. Arrested, produced before a magistrate, he pleaded that the matter was extremely urgent and he barely got into the train running. When questioned about the urgency-emergency situation, he informed that he had an uncanny ability to foresee disastrous events in as much as he had a premonition that Glasgow may be rocked by a severe earthquake any time soon, and therefore he had to rush to the Met Department in London so that they could forewarn the public of the impending disaster. The jury found no reason to believe this hotchpotch story and convicted Edward of dual crime of ticketless travel and misleading the court. Exactly three weeks after this trial news of the earthquake and forewarning by Edward made headlines in the media. No doubt our past and future are closely related to the present, albeit indirectly.

All prophecies are precognition, but all precognitions are not prophecies in as much as that the divine inspiration is an essential element of prophecies while it is not so in the case of precognitions. However, there is no such distinction between a prophecy and prediction.

References

1. William Flexner: *An Introduction to Parapsychology;* p. 108
2. Raymond Buckland: *The Encyclopedia of Clairvoyance, Channeling, and Spirit Communication, Canton*; USA, 2005; p. 318

8

Dreams

Dreams are the language of the soul,
and because we dream every night,
it is important we learn this language.
– Ruth Montgomery

We dream only when we are asleep. Day dreaming is a different matter altogether. When we are asleep, even in deep slumber, it is only the conscious mind that becomes silent and inactive; the subconscious and unconscious minds generally continue their work in the inner and subliminal domains— of a very high quality; a stimulus affecting the mind without the subject being aware of it. Our unconscious mind does not really sleep or relax. It continues to update its memory and resetting the mental processing in the brain. However, the capabilities of our conscious mind are quite limited. It cannot grasp the unexpressed knowledge nor can it "conceptualise the subliminal facets of Nature." These are unexplained enigmas of the nature of our Mind. Perhaps, it would be easier to explain this via a small story:

A British hunter was out hunting tigers near the ruins of an ancient temple in the thick forests of Sapigehalli village in Shimoga district of Karnataka.

After a quick reconnaissance he found that the temple-ruins provided the best hiding place waiting for his prey during the hours of darkness. Before long a tiger appeared near the well around midnight. While the hunter was focusing his gun to shoot, a sudden exceptionally melodious whistling sound emanated from the well that distracted the hunter's aim. After a few moments he saw the tiger sitting at the same spot in the same position and took aim. Before he could press the trigger the melodious whistling sound again distracted his aim. A few moments later the tiger jumped into the well. The hunter too felt as if the whistling sound was pulling him also into the well! Terrified and horrified beyond belief, the brave British hunter ran back towards the village and narrated his mysterious tale of woe to the rustic people well before dawn. They informed him that this mysterious incident occurs every year on that particular night in which a number of hunters have lost their lives; he was lucky to escape being sucked into the well, and to be alive at that moment. Incidentally, a somewhat similar story is associated with Chama Nath in the valley of Nilgiri Hills in South India during the historic times of Tipu Sultan when Captain Ned of British Army in India was out on a similar hunt. While resting at night in the temple, a mysterious brass lamp suddenly became lighted. The Captain was fascinated and took the lamp home. That was his undoing. He became seriously ill and doctors were at a loss about the nature of affliction. The villagers told his wife to return the lamp to its original location soon after which the Captain was his usual self again.

Our conscious mind plays the principal role of experiencing and understanding the gross perceivable world, while totally neglecting the remaining 93 per cent potential of the Mind. The great yogis and masters of spirituality of the East perceive the transcendental as well as the gross world beyond any barrier of time by activating the latent intellect.[1/2]

Some people are gifted with an uncanny ability to have prophetic dreams in as much as their dreams foretell an event not yet occurred. There are numerous case histories on record, the most noteworthy of which is the dream Abraham Lincoln (1809-1865), the 16th President of the United States, had about his own death besides some other prophetic dreams.

In 1858 the Clemens Brothers, Sam and Henry, were training to be river boat captains of steam boat paddle wheelers. After they anchored at St Louis they went to their sister's place for a visit. After dinner Henry went back to the Boat but Sam stayed on with the sister. As Sam was sliding off to sleep he dreamt his brother's body was in a casket balanced across two chairs, flowers sprayed across the casket, a cascade of white roses with a single red rose in the center of the bloom. Sam returned to the Boat next morning; but they were again separated when Sam had to go on another Boat. Three days later the Boat in which Henry had left behind exploded due to boiler accident and all 150 on board were killed. Sam left his boat, hired a horse and rushed to Memphis, the site of accident, and found Henry's body in a metal casket, balanced across two chairs. A volunteer nurse walked over to the casket and laid across it a bouquet of white roses with one single red rose in its center.

Our dreams are memories of journeys made by our 'astral body' during our sleep when the spirit may go to any part of the universe but still remain attached to the physical body on Planet Earth through the medium of 'silver chord'. Astral Projection is essentially Out-Of-Body-Experience (OBE). It is somewhat similar to Extra-Sensory Perception (ESP), an umbrella term which covers such phenomena as telepathy, clairvoyance, clairsentience, precognition, psychokinesis, et al. Dreams are a primary venue for spirit communication, especially for people who are tuned into psychic forces, Lucid dreams are nocturnal images with a high degree of clarity and content.In fact, numerous instances of dreams of death of close friends/relatives coming true have been recorded from all over the globe in the past 2-3 centuries. In some cases even animals too have supernormal faculties lying dormant in their brains. Such beings may just wither away, or in some exceptional cases, these dormant faculties become activated due to some abnormal accidental stimulation of some extra-sensory centers in the brain. The case of a Russian crane operator, who received a massive electrical shock while driving the crane, was declared almost dead and sent for postmortem, when doctors noticed a faint activity in her brain. With intensive care she recovered and came back to life. Now she could see much deeper and sharper than normal human beings. She developed X-ray vision in her naked eyes. She could see hidden sources of water, minerals below the surface of the earth. She became a star attraction for scientific curiosity and research. Obviously, the strong electrical shock had activated quite a few extra-sensory functions in her brain. The case was thoroughly examined and verified by world renowned experts in parapsychology.[3]

As late as in the 1950's my own Father-in-Law took his own young son in his tender teens out for an evening walk. He was in his early 50's and told his son that after he goes away from this mortal world, his ashes should be taken to Haridwar for immersion in the sacred River Ganges in Northern India. The ashes should be accompanied by his wife and eldest son who was not in location at that time. On hearing this sad advice, the youngster started crying, sobbing loudly. My Father-in-Law told him not to worry about this matter at all and that he just happened to mention Green C.E.: Lucid Dreams, London 1968.

Jung CG: Dreams; Princeton 1974; Man His Symbols, 1964 this to him in passing, more as a pass time story, and not at all serious. Since my Father-in-Law was in good health and not at all old, the youngster accepted the explanation and became calm.

Unfortunately, my Father-in-Law passed away a couple of weeks later. A couple of days earlier he had mentioned to his wife about a strange dream. But since he was in excellent health this dream story did not cause much excitement. However, when his ashes after cremation were being carried away for immersion by his younger brother, the youngster in his teens started crying and sobbing, and insisted that his Mother and elder Brother must accompany the ashes. It is not customary for Hindu ladies to go for immersion of ashes. But the young boy insisted. On being questioned he related the story of his evening walk with his late Father.

Dreams have been a puzzle to mankind since ancient times. Dreams were thought to be supernatural events as messages from gods, predictions and divinations. In Greek tradition the right dream in the Temple of Aesculapius, the god of healing, implied that it was the right cure.

A comprehensive system of dream interpretation was developed in the 2nd Century A.D. and remained in force till Sigmund Freud's time. Until then, dreams were considered as the means of communication by the spirits with human beings. Whether the dreamer can recall what he dreamt or not is immaterial, since every element of the dream has some significance or the other to various issues and events connected with the life of the dreamer. Dreams may be paranormal, clairvoyant, precognitive or telepathic. Others may be connected with past life experience. In lucid dreams the dreamer is aware of the dream and may even alter its outcome. Dreams are conditioned by age, sex, occupation and station in life of the dreamer. However, during the Middle Ages the Church preached that dreams should be ignored. Perhaps, the Church wanted to ensure that that institution alone was the ultimate authority in all matters concerning humans. It was the reformation period that brought an end to belief in miracles and supernatural events. Nevertheless, dreams continued to hold their position in the lives of humans although psychological explanations were not given to dreams till Sigmund Freud produced his path-breaking work in 1900, The Interpretation of Dreams. He made us believe that dreams were wish-fulfillment of repressed infantile desires.

On the other hand Psychiatrist Carl G. Jung considered "dreams as the expression of contents of the personal and collective unconscious." Outsiders cannot interpret a dream's true meaning; only the dreamer can. Be that as it may, we must not, and cannot afford to, ignore the significance of our dreams. There is always a meaning behind every dream, albeit one may not be able to recall it accurately.

Dreams occur during the REM (Rapid Eye Movement) stages of sleep. A typical seven-hour sleep of a healthy person is divided into 60-90 minutes cycles, each cycle having a certain period of REM during which dreams occur. The initial cycle may have the minimum REM period of 5-10 minutes while the final one, just before waking, may be as long as forty minutes. That is the one most people seem to remember. Unless you write down your dream story immediately, most dreams fade away in 5-10 minutes. Infants dream more than the adults.

Animals also dream. Dreams do have colors but no smell or taste. Dreams are also a source of inspiration for creativity. Ideas for inventions, problem-solving, poetry, artistic expressions all find their way to human intellect via the dreams. Not that all these creative activities come only through dreams; far from it. Nevertheless, dreams do play a significant role in this direction. In the same vein all dreams do not have a positive element; some are negative too. They are the barometers of good and bad health. Dreams prepare terminally ill to prepare for death via "transitional dreams". Then you have paranormal dreams that have a certain degree of prophetic content. Certain symbols or emotions accompany such dreams to enable a dreamer to distinguish grain from the husk. They could be spontaneous or telepathic too. Telepathy has been scientifically established a fact of life in dreams.

Lucidity occurs in varying degrees in lucid dreams. At the lowest level one awakes from a lucid dream and realises that it was merely a dream. On the other side of the scale, one is aware of the dream as it progresses and can influence its course and or outcome. Generally speaking, lucid dreams are characterised by light, mellow or bright, intense emotions, heightened colors, images, levitation, et al. "Sex plays a prominent role in lucid dreams, especially for women."

References

1. Based on *Extrasensory Potential of the Mind*, in the Author's own words, p. 113
2. *Ibid,*
3. Pandit Shriram Sharma Acharya: *Extra Sensory Potential of the Mind*; Shri Vedmata Gyatri Trust, Haridwar; p. 53.

9

Ghosts and Apparitions

Ghosts and apparitions mean one and the same thing. The former is a rather crude expression while the psychiatrists and psychotherapists use the more refined phrase, 'apparitions'. Hundreds of cases of apparitions of living people have been recorded in *Phantasms of the Living.*[1] Ghosts are humans, and in some odd case, may be animals too, or even inanimate objects like cars, airplanes or trains. Apparitions' profligate in damp conditions which probably explains why England with its notorious climate has more ghosts per square mile than any other country in the world. A tingling feeling is generally experienced by the person(s) who encounter an apparition. Every person who transits to the "Other Side" generally passes through the 'tunnel of light' at the end of which the entity is finally sent where it belongs.

Some odd souls who have left behind some unfulfilled strong desires, like unfulfilled love, heavy uncollected debt, etc. they do not follow the normal path and stay behind in this mortal world as stray souls, as ghosts. The place where they stay is said to be haunted -- a house, a tree, a castle, woods, garden, cave, and so on. Many ghosts haunt particular places for their personal reasons in their just extinguished lives. Traumatic experience or extreme happiness in that particular place may be the primary cause of such attachment. The large haunted house built by Rev. Henry Bull in 1860 is the most notorious example of ghastly activity than anywhere else. Whenever séances were held in that House, there used to be rapping, apparitions, pebbles flying all over the place, keys pushed out of the locks, and what have you as similar phenomena.

Existence or belief in ghosts goes a long way to strengthen our belief in life after death, survival of death. So does ancestor worship that ties us down to beliefs in ghosts. In some religions ancestor worship assumes power of minor gods.

Celia Green: *Apparitions*; London 1975

Guiley, Rosemary Allen: The Encyclopedia of Ghosts and Spirits; New York, Facts on File, 1992, New York.

Harpers Encyclopedia of Mystical and Paranormal Experience, 1991, San Francisco

When we see a ghost, which many often do, we see them as clothed. But cloth is inanimate. It does not have any after life and therefore is not the material of the other-side; so why do we see the apparitions as clothed. Of course they are not clothed from the other world! It is our mind that clothes them as we see them since we are used to seeing our loved ones as dressed as they used to be. Spirits play games with us, so do our minds too. Nonetheless, a scholarly definition of a ghost is worth quoting: "A manifestation of persistent energy, or an indication that some kind of force is being exercised after death which in some way is connected with a person previously known on earth."[2]

Clairaudience is the phenomenon of being able to clearly hear the sound and voices of spirits of the dead during a Séance. Cult of the dead was, and still is, widespread amongst communities with ties to the ancient past. Most communities of the East and some like the Egyptians, Greeks, Siberians, Amerindians, Intuits, etc. in the west are strong believers-practitioners of cult of the dead, and in life after death. Immortality of the soul is an important part of their religious belief system. Most of them also believed, and still do, that the "Etheric Double" or 'ultra-gaseous body' acts as a vital sheath for the physical body; as a copy of the physical entity - "Prana" or "Linga Sharira" in Hindu yoga-practice. The by-product of this system of beliefs came out to be belief in ghosts and apparitions. However, ghosts do not cause us any harm. In fact, they are not able to cause any harm to living beings. It is the fear of the unexpected that is the root cause of our problem with the ghosts.

Occasionally, ghosts are known to have been harbingers of death, advance messengers of Yama Raja if I may so. It is believed that ghost of Josephine appeared before Napoleon some days before he died. She came as a signal, advance warning of his impending death. And that holds good for Lord Byron's family when a Black Friar is said to have appeared.[3]

Using Electronic Voice Phenomena (EVP) and Instrumental Trans Communication (ITC), radios, tape recorders, telephones, computers, video equipment, answering machines, et al --- the spirits of the dead from the land of the dead have communicated with our mortal world via some of these devices through appropriate mediums. Radio contact with the land of the dead started way back in 1967. Tens of thousands of voices of deceased persons have been recorded and catalogued by spiritualists-scientists. Parapsychologists have done this under strict laboratory conditions so as not to leave any grounds for doubt. No wonder therefore that "Ancestor-Worship" is prevalent in various parts of the world as an occult practice. It represents religious awareness of belief in ghosts. It is a philosophical system for the attainment of the higher powers of the mind and spirit. Generally speaking, ghosts do not cause us any harm although their appearance may be frightening --- "Fear of the Unknown". Our loved ones may not be with us any longer in this world but still they continue to be concerned about us and do play some role in our lives on Planet Earth. Death is not a terminus; it is merely a transition from one state to another. Our elders continue to live in another world and send us messages via the spirit mediums.

The communications received from the spirit world through the agencies of the medium(s) are known as messages. These are transmitted to us in the mortal world through the medium's clairvoyance (clear-seeing), clairaudience (clear-hearing) clairsentience (clear-sensing), rapping, auto-writing, slate writing, table-tipping, etc. However, the frequency on which the spirit world operates is different from that of our physical world. The former is higher than the latter; hence the need for suitable mediums to effect communication. To put this in another way: there is life after death.

Metaphysically[4] speaking, the human body is composed of seven distinct elements:

- Solid, liquid and gas form the basic physical body;
- The fourth element, the Ethereal (Celestial, Heavenly, unworldly) Body interpenetrates the physical body;
- The Astral (Visionary or Exalted) Body;
- The Mental body;
- The Spiritual body.

The last three are non-physical elements that go to make up the human body in its entirety. The physical body may have died but the spirit continues to live. The sitters in the séance experience a sense of relief and comfort in that those gone-by are keeping a watch on them and that they are themselves comfortable in their new abode. Phantom phone calls from the dead relatives purported to have been received by many people have lent credence to the idea of communications between the land of the dead and this mortal world. Communication with spirit world is effected thru spirit guide(s). A spiritual medium may have more than one guide. Innumerable cases of radio contact between the deceased persons and their loved ones in this world have been reported from the Western world, but none from the East.

Numerous instances of messages received from deceased loved ones have been noted in various parts of the world. They intercede on behalf of their loved ones when the latter may be in serious danger, or when they require guidance to stick to the right path. It is generally the mothers or grandparents who appear as apparitions for the benefit of their young ones. Sometimes they give advance notice of coming events, mostly death, and sometimes births and pregnancies too. The possibility of developing an electromagnetic-etheric-communication system that would enable human beings to have telephone-like conversation with those in the land of the dead is the eventual goal of spiritualist community. Incidentally, Lily Dale, New York, is the oldest and largest spiritualist community in the world. Psychics do get things right. Spiritualist churches are found all over Europe, America and some parts of the Middle East too.

The institution of angels, meaning messengers, is prevalent in most religions in one form or the other. Angels are generally noble in character but some angels could be bad. The helping angels are known by various terms: 'Guardian angels', 'guardian spirit', 'tutelary spirit', 'protective spirit', etc. The Buddhist angels are like demigods and are known as *devas*, meaning "shining ones". In the Old Testament there are many references to angels acting as "messengers of God". In Islam there are two angels for every person: one to record the good deeds and the other the bad ones. Further, Islam has an angel of death known as *Azreal* besides an angel of destruction called *Asrafil*. They are equipped with whips, iron rods and fire. In this connection those well versed in Christian theology would recall Lucifer, an angel of the New Testament who defied God and was therefore thrown out of heaven along with his followers all of whom later became demons of hell while their leader Lucifer was renamed as the Satan.

In 1978 Esther was eighteen, had a handsome but rather unstable young man as boyfriend by name Bob Mclean who had tried to rape her. They parted. In September Esther was in bed with Jennie and started crying admitting that she was thinking of Bob. Soon after going to sleep again she screamed saying that there was mouse in the bed. Search revealed nothing. The episode was repeated the next night also. The rustling seemed to come from a box under the bed. So the box was placed outside and suddenly the box rose about a foot in the air. The next night Esther leapt out of bed, screaming and grinding her teeth, shouting she was dying. Her body seemed to be swelling. There was a loud thunderclap from under the bed and her body stopped swelling and she went back to sleep. Three nights later Esther again felt the body swelling, her bed linen flew off followed by loud bangs after which Esther deflated and fell asleep. Next night a doctor was called. He declared that she was suffering from shock. At that moment the pillow inflated like a balloon, bedclothes flew off and wrapping noises were heard. An invisible claw scratched deep into the wall above: "Esther Cox, you are mine to kill". All present were terrified. Esther was given morphia but loud bangs from atop the roof started as if someone was pounding on the roof with a sledge hammer. Three weeks later Esther went into a trance and told the story of attempted rape.

In January 1879 a voice told Esther that the house would be burned down. Lighted match sticks rained on the bed and all over the bedroom. All were extinguished. One of her dresses was found burning under the bed. Later, a barrel full of wood-shavings was found burning. A kind neighbor took Esther to their home. Poltergeist activity was signaled when a scrubbing brush flew through the air. While on work in a restaurant she was attacked by a flying jackknife, burning hot spikes were placed on her lap and she was returned to her home when loud wrappings were heard on the main street of Amherst. Esther claimed she saw ghosts one of whom was her old boy friend, Bob Nickle.

A magician confirmed that the spirits were responsible for mystery. So she was sent to a farm to work where she was accused of theft and arson and jailed for four months when all poltergeist activity ceased.

Another case at Rosenheim has close similarities with the Amherst episode. Here again the focus was on Anne-Marie Schabrel, a bored dissatisfied girl in her late teens. Soon after leaving school in 1965 she went to work in office of an attorney, Sigmund Adam at Rosenheim near Munich. Two years on, the office started having problems with electrical systems. Strip lights kept falling. Sudden inexplicable surges in current became routine. All checks and investigations proved fruitless. For instance, when a voltmeter was connected to a 1.5V battery, it registered three volts; normally impossible. Telephone bill of the outfit came to six times the normal. Someone must be getting straight to the relay! An investigative journalist visited the site and a bulb fell straight on his head out of the socket. The story somehow reached the ears of Professor Hans Bender of Paranormal Research at Freiburg. His assistant discovered that it was probably Anne Marie who was the raison d'être for the problem. It was noticed that whenever she walked up and down the corridor the lights began to swing back and forth. And when she was not in the office premises, everything was normal as usual.

Soon the poltergeist became more active. Pictures on walls turned; lights swung, changing direction midway between. A heavy filing cabinet in the hall was moved away from the wall. Anne-Marie was given leave of absence and sent to Bender Institute where they found her to be typical of the personality that causes poltergeist phenomena. Bender put her on ESP tests and she showed remarkable telepathic abilities. When she returned to her old office poltergeist was active as before. She got a new job, but poltergeist activity persisted. Her fiancé broke off the relationship. She married someone else, moved out of Rosenheim and had three children. Poltergeist activity ceased and life was back to normal.

Has Bender's final conclusion: Anne-Marie was a case of spontaneous PK --- Psychokinesis.

Guiley Rosemary Ellen: *Encyclopedia of the Strange*

A number of well attested verified cases of "human batteries" have been recorded. Two most noteworthy besides the above are:

Caroline Clare of Bandon, Ontario, was seventeen when she started wasting without any reason. She was down to 90 lbs from a healthy 130 earlier. Seizures began. The body became rigid. After slow recovery she turned into a human battery. Anyone who touched her got an electric shock. Pieces of iron stuck to her and had to be physically pulled out of her skin by force. However, the 'battery syndrome' disappeared when she grew out of her teens. In another similar case fourteen-years-old Jennie Morgan of Sedalia, Missouri, started generating enough electric power in 1895 to knock out flat even a grown up man. In her case too, the problem disappeared as she reached maturity. Yet another case of human battery in

Missouri was rather peculiar in as much as the lad developed the electric charge during the night but gradually lost the same as the day wore on. The most interesting thing about this young man was that when electrically charged, his feet stuck to the ground and walking became difficult.[5]

When I was working as a Project Manager at San'? in Yemen one of my colleagues, an engineer from Bengal, was often electrically charged. Merely touching him just by chance generally gave a mild shock. We used to discuss this often amongst our group and concluded that the dry climate of the region and altitude of the place, rather high, combined to have that effect on that man. May be, might not be. However, we hardly had any spare time to devote to such extraneous matters...

On the other side of the coin is the ghost. Ghosts are galore in folklore, literature and art of all nations of the world. Parapsychologists prefer the more sophisticated term "apparition". It is an apparition of a person or animal which is not physically present at that point of time and space. A noisy ghost is called poltergeist. It is a manifestation of persistent personal energy. The phenomena of raps on walls, roofs, windows and furniture are typical of poltergeist activities. A ghost does not necessarily represent a dead entity; it could well be like a normal solid being. Ghosts are not necessarily apparitions of human beings; these could well be of animals, and even inanimate objects like airplane, train, coaches, etc. The existence of Ghosts goes a long way in strengthening our belief in life after death. Survival after death is the crux of phenomenon of ghosts.

Since these images or apparitions do not exist in reality they give rise to fear and are connected with horror stories. However, apparitions of religious figures are in a different class by themselves and are welcomed as visions of the sacred. Similarly, apparitions of loved ones do come as a pleasant surprise. The case of Mary Todd Lincoln having her picture being taken in a professional studio is well known. This was soon after President Lincoln was assassinated. When the picture was developed, the late President was clearly seen in the picture standing behind her chair. It was the spirit, an apparition of the late President that made its appearance behind his wife. This episode is somewhat like an apport: something brought on the scene by a spirit. Apport and asport (opposite of apport: disappearance of something) are common features in some séances, spiritual gatherings.

Since the Lincoln-episode "spirit-photography" gained recognition and many 'spirit photographers' have taken pictures in which the spirit of a close relation of the person being photographed makes an appearance. The image of the spirit which makes the appearance is thus retained on the developed picture as a permanent record. The experiences of Emma Ada Deane, a well known spirit-photographer, and his companion, Dr. Hereward Carrington, during the 1920's throw interesting light on such strange episodes.

A more or less similar experience of Baron L. De Guldenstubbé (1820-1873) who found mysterious writings on some papers he had kept in a locked box add credence to the phenomena of spirits proving their existence in the mortal world. In fact, the latter claimed that when he left the box open with just the blank paper only, he saw the letters being formed without even a pencil being used. In a similar case a young student who could not write an essay as part of her assignment and went to sleep crying. She left the paper she had picked for the work on her bed side table. When she woke up next morning she was totally flabbergasted to find the writing on the blank paper, all in her own hand writing — an excellent essay which impressed her teacher and the faculty. The young student happened to be Elizabeth Hope (1855-1919).

Spirits do play 'games' with us in the mortal world. Strange things happen in haunted houses. The spirit(s) occupying the house may indulge in knockings and rapping which can be quite scary for the occupants of the house. However, if the people in the house have the patience and are not afraid, they can communicate with the spirit by asking questions and receiving answers in the manner requested. Belief in spiritualism is a pre-requisite for communicating with the spirit world. If a person has been murdered in a house, his spirit may continue to remain in the house and provide information about the events leading to the murder and details about the accused person(s).

Strange things also do happen in places which are not haunted! — Alan Whites was a gifted intelligent highly religious person well versed in Eastern religions and theology, particularly of Buddhism. At age 20 he wrote his first book: *The Spirit of Zen: A Way of Life, Work and Art in the Far East*, a very difficult and complicated subject at best. He was a philosopher and religious teacher of repute having done his Masters degree in Theology and Doctorate in Divinity, besides having been ordained as an Anglican priest in 1944 and also served as Episcopal Chaplain in North Western University in Evanston for six years. He married Eleanor in 1936 and found Ruth Everett, his first mother-in-law very well versed in Zen.

After Eleanor gave him two daughters, Watts married their baby-sitter, Dorothy De Witt in 1950. He was then excommunicated. In 1963 while in California, where he was professor of philosophy in at American Academy of Asian Studies, he married Mary Jones Yates, now for the third time. His sexual escapades, extramarital affairs, excessive indulgence in tobacco and alcohol besides drugs, were the crux of his philosophy of his personal life. His health deteriorated considerably. Nonetheless, he experimented with Zen breathing techniques to attain Samadhi, a state of enlightenment of the higher self. In a way he was a debauch yet was gifted with occult-psychic powers. He died age 58. Stories of strange Incidents circulated after his death. According to one, the great gong of Druid Heights in San Francisco sounded on its own at the time of death of Watts. When alive he had predicted that he would return to that site as a lightning flash, which he did on December 21, the night of the winter solstice that knocked out an underground cable on the lane leading to Druid Heights. "Watts sexual and sensual appetites were in keeping with the Tantric mystical tradition" though he lacked the self discipline to moderate his behaviour.[6]

It is well known that in the past the Western philosophy did not accept the Eastern versions of occult practices, spiritualism, after-life, ghosts and haunted houses, etc. This mental block has now given way to open acceptance of OBE, NDE, Astral Projection, etc. In so far as the Americans are concerned they have readily accepted these occult practices as part and parcel of life. For instance: A Gallup Poll held in 1980 revealed that 71 per cent of Americans believe in Life after Death while a similar Poll held in 2001 showed that 38 per cent of them believe that it is possible to make contact with the dead. Going a step further, 42 per cent of Americans believe in ghosts and haunting.

Ghosts may be there and a place may be haunted but it is not necessary that everyone who visits the place would perceive a ghost. That indeed is the characteristic of ghosts and haunting. Most Britons believe that UFOs do exist. In fact, nine per cent of them insist that they have seen a UFO one time or the other while 43 per cent of them believe in alien life. The US survey involved 7,123 cases in which death day apparitions occurred at 487 times the rate predicted by chance. In the British survey of 17,000 cases the result was 442.6 times. Chances of any person dying on a given day were 1 in 19000. The survey was conducted by International Congress of Experimental Psychology in Aug 1892 to find out chances of apparitions to occur the same day.

The foregoing statistics just show a major transformation in mental make-up of Western minds during the past half century. And Tibetan Diaspora has given an added fill-up to this belief system. Thanks to the Chinese for pulling out the Western Civilisation from its exalted ignorance ... While bad is bad but not that bad that no good may come out of it!

References

1. Published by Gurney, Myers and Podmore, the three founding members of the Society for Psychical Research; 1886
2. Frederick W.H. Myers, Founder of the Society for Psychical Research
   Evans-Wentz W.Y.: *Tibetan Yoga and Secret Doctrines*; Oxford University Press, 1969
3. Raymond Buckland:*The Spirit Book*: *The Encyclopedia of Clairvoyance, Channeling, and Spirit Communication*; Visible Ink, Detroit, 2005; p. 162.
   Echo Bodine: *Relax It's Only a Ghost;* Element, Boston, 2000
4. Relating to transcendental, or to a reality beyond what is perceptible to the senses
5. Collin Wilson: op. cit. p. 268-69.
6. Emmons Charles: *Chinese Ghosts and ESP*; New Jersey.
   Andrew MacKenzie: *Haunting and Apparitions*; London, 1982.
   Monica Furlong: *Zen Effects: The Life of Alan Watts*; New York 1986.
   Also: *Selected Writings of Gopi Krishna*; New York 1988.

10

Near Death Experience (NDE) Out of Body Experience (OBE)

The term "Near Death experience" (NDE) was coined in 1970 by the American physician-psychiatrist Raymond Moody, in the course of his paranormal research. However, the phenomenon of NDE has been known for centuries, perhaps for as long as the history of religion. It is comparable with "Out-of-Body-Experience" (OBE) also known as 'astral projections' although there are subtle differences between the two concepts. OBEs are brief, bizarre incidents involving a sensation of floating outside one's physical body. Such experiences must not be confused with drugs induced hallucinations. OBEs are generally induced when an individual is under intense emotional pressure or stress. Such an experience may last up to about fifteen minutes, generally less.

OBE's have been induced through electrical stimulation also. The idea is shrouded in mysticism in as much as Hindu sages, Tibetan spiritualists, Sufi masters, and besides some monks from Western monasteries have dwelt on the subject from time to time. A number of such cases have been well researched and documented proving beyond any doubt the veracity of statements made by survivours and narrators of their OBE. While most NDE's have reported positive pleasant experiences in the far distance well away from the site of their near-death, the OBE's have generally talked about dream like experience of floating in the close vicinity of their human frame, and viewing their body and its environment from somewhere above. While under the influence of OBE they have a clear consciousness, their sense organs are fully alert, in fact may be even heightened having the ability to overcome physical obstacles like walls, roofs, etc.

NDE got a big boost from medical technologies and successful application of skills by the medico-psychiatrists professionals. As a result a number of people who would normally have been consigned to graves/flames were revived from a state of near death to tell fantastic tales of their experiences of bright dazzling luminosity, or long dark tunnels opening into strong visible light at the end. Bright dazzling blinding light which did no harm to the eyes has been a common denominator of most recitals of NDE. At first they, perhaps their soul-force, see a point-light to which they are involuntarily attracted and soon get enveloped in magnificent light and love. Telepathy is the common medium of communication while time and space are no constraints at all. Some of them soon reach a boundary beyond which it is 'out of bounds'; they cannot proceed further. Here they might meet one of their loved ones, a dead ancestor of old days, or even some recently died close relation.

While most NDE descriptions are pleasant and happy, a few terrifying of hellish realms have also been recorded where the subject experiences terror, fear, panic, loneliness, desolation and gloom. Intense cold, heat and burning have also been reported by some while others have reported of being sucked into "a vast black vortex like whirlpool". Angie Fennimore[1] has given a vividly terrifying description of her NDE, in her book on the subject. To go a step further: Sogyal Rinpoche has recorded a very interesting one in a billion case of a Tibetan female 'delok' (means returned from death) who was sent back to the world, as there had been an error about her name and family, and that it was not yet time for her to die. She returned to her body, recovered, and spent the rest of her allotted time in the mortal world. Thank God she was not in America otherwise the Angels of Death would have had to pay hefty damages for their mistake! The lives of such experiences of NDE are generally transformed into loving sublime human beings.

As it is, the East has been known to believe in NDE since ancient times. What is surprising is that the numbers of Westerners who have come to accept the reality of NDE have grown many folds. According to a report published in the Times of India New Delhi dated July 16, 200722 and the 1981-82 Gallup Poll about eight million Americans have had at least one NDE/OBE experience in their lifetime. However, it is noteworthy that nature and description of NDE differs considerably from person to person ... Most have been good ones but many have been negative too.

Dr. Raymond Moody has done pioneering work in this field and his celebrated book Life After Life is a classic devoted to this topic. Patients, who have suffered near fatal crisis in their life, or have undergone life saving surgery and have recovered, describe their personal experience as if they have had an "inspirational glimpse" beyond the grave. Their experiences are consistent and surprisingly follow the same set pattern:

- Self-visualisation from a higher position;
- Passage into an unknown foreign region or dimension;
- A combination of the above two states.

After the spirit has left the physical body self-visualisation is indeed astral projection at the end of which the patient can recollect various details of the surgery besides remembering the conversations that took place between the surgical staff and the doctors. Since the patient has returned from the jaws of death he generally describes vividly the process of near death, and all that transpired in that state of his body and soul.

Most patients felt that as a first step they were enveloped in total darkness, in utterly black dark void. The darkness was so deep and impenetrable that I just could not see anything else.[3] They had the sensation of being rapidly pulled through a sort of dark tunnel. They were somewhat conscious of their surroundings and had a peculiar feeling of peace and lightness. Most of them also saw a being of bright shining light at the end of the tunnel, but it was not a dazzling uncomfortable light; indeed it was a welcome pleasant change. In the process most witnessed flashing scenes from their past life. After sometime some of them were told in a stern commanding voice to get back in there, and they immediately found themselves back in their original physical body. Hereafter their life was completely transformed. Materialism gave way to spiritualism, far more relaxed and peaceful.

In 1944 the renowned analytical-psychologist, Carl Gustav Jung (1875-1961), had a near-death experience following a heart attack. As he lay in bed, a nurse observed him surrounded by a bright halo of light. She had earlier observed a similar phenomenon around other patients who were dying. However, Jung recovered, and later recounted what happened to him during that time. He felt he was floating high over the Earth and could see from the Himalayas across the Middle East to a part of the Mediterranean. He became aware that he was leaving the Earth. Then he saw near him a huge block of stone that had been hollowed out into a temple. He saw a black Hindu, sitting in a lotus position, to the right of the temple entrance. Jung felt that he was expected inside the temple. As he reached closer to the temple-entrance, he felt all his earthly desires and attitudes falling away from him and he became aware that when inside he would understand the real meaning of his life. Just at that very moment his earthy doctor appeared in the form of the Basileus of Kos, the healer at the temple of Aesculapius, the Roman god of healing, telling him that he had to return to Earth. Jung did so most reluctantly and with great resentment against his doctor. He knew the doctor was going to die because he had manifested in what Jung interpreted as his primal form. And the doctor did die soon thereafter.

Following this episode Jung experienced a remarkable transformation in which he felt he was in the happy state experienced by the unborn. He had vision in which he was Adam and a Jew while his nurse was his Magna Mater (Mater=Mother) who proceeded to teach him the mystery of the Eros Gamos, or 'sacred marriage' with the Divine.

Shamanism too held a version of NDE as one of their myths. A Shaman hero passes through the gates of death only to return with a lesson for the living. Modern NDE narratives enable the believers to incorporate a "religious sense of the cosmos" into their secular/scientific understanding. In fact, NDE is a form of enlightenment or a "gateway to a higher consciousness". It is conjectured that NDE could have a transformative effect on the entire planet if enough people on Earth could have that sort of experience --- excellent idea but nonetheless a mere conjecture only.

From the foregoing discussion the following conclusions emerge:

- Most of the NDE experiences are positive. Barely 3 per cent happen to be negative or unpleasant;

- NDE is not limited to religious or good people only. However, most NDE returnees do turn out to be more spiritual with strong belief in God;
- Most NDE returnees lose fear of death and start believing in after-life;
- Most returnees are spiritually transformed and find a positive purpose in their life;
- Some returnees develop heightened intuitive or psychic abilities like precognition, clairvoyance, telepathy, etc.;
- In her 1988 study of after-effects of NDE (Coming Back to Life) M.H. Atwater found that anger was the most common negative reaction amongst survivours of NDE for the simple reason that they had to come back to same work and place, which was rather disappointing and depressive. They also suffered from guilt complex for having left their dear ones behind.
- In short, all is not hunky dory with NDE as has been propagated all along!

References

1. Angie Fennimore: *Beyond the Darkness: My Near Death Experience to the Edge of Hell and Back*
2. Gallup and Proctor: Adventures in Immortality, 1982 ... 15 per cent Americans reported having had an NDE experience while 42 per cent of those polled claimed to have had contact with the dead.
3. Moody A. Raymond: Life After Life; Rider, 1975; p. 22.

11
Hindu Tradition

As opposed to all other religions of the entire world, Hinduism has no Founder, no defining Creed, and no centralised hierarchy. It is vast, subtle and complex, world-defining and world-denying. The oldest documents-scriptures of Hinduism are the Vedas (Sacred Teachings) compiled around 1000 B.C. to 500 B.C. Thus they are the oldest extant religious literature in the world and, of course, the oldest religious literature in an Indo-European language. The Vedas are still held to contain the essential truths of Hinduism. Vedas are believed to be of divine origin and are the literature of the Aryans who invaded India in the second millennium B.C.

Vedas are divided into four books the oldest of which is the Rig Veda. All four Vedas serve as manuals for priests for prayers, meditational practices, as hymns and chanting during magical rites, etc. They were the essential part of the Aryan sacrificial cult. Vedas recognised gods who were considered the great super-powers of nature and phenomena in their own respective fields. However, these gods did not have the power to aid humans in their spiritual endeavours.

The Upanishads are the next generation of ancient sacred Hindu scriptures. They are called the last part of the Vedas, Vedanta, end of the Vedas, the Vedic period. They are essentially philosophical compilations, highly intellectual and a reflection of advancement of Hindu thought and philosophy in those ancient times when the West was immersed deep in ignorance. Their compilation began in c. 900 B.C. and represents the earliest systematic collection of mystical and monastic Hindu religious literature. By this time self- renunciation had come to be the accepted path to spiritual ecstasy and enlightenment. Asceticism thus took roots in Hindu psyche and also spread the concept to other parts of Asia. In some cases it took the form of self-mortification too. The extreme forms of such practices included lying on a bed of spikes, continuously gazing at the sun, holding up an arm till it is withered away, hanging from trees in an upside-down posture, etc.

The Upanishad introduced the concept of the One *Brahm* (One Supreme Being) as successor to numerous Vedic gods and goddesses, besides the concept of ineffable cosmic, all that holds all things together and unifies all life. The concept of Brahman is unique to Hinduism. He is the one Reality and the eternal Absolute. It is Brahman who brings all things into existence, supports them, and reabsorbs them in the endless cycle of birth-death-rebirth, called *Samsara*, that is determined by Karma, the principle of cause and effect liberation from which is possible only through union with Brahm — the Omnipresent Supreme Consciousness manifests itself as Mãyã — the physical world, the perceivable world, the perceptible expression of Nature. Mâyâ is ultimately absorbed in the Brahm. This is the esoteric Vedanta Philosophy.

The Brahm is also identified with Atman, the immortal part of the self, the eternal soul, indestructible, absolute bliss and absolute consciousness. Hindu philosophy identifies the self, the soul and Brahman by simply saying "Ahm Brahm Asmi" (I am Brahm) "tat twm asi" (that thou art). This thought is so deep and meaningful that most find it difficult to fathom its significance. Indeed Brahman is beyond comprehension, whose three manifestations are the Creator, Shiva (the sustainer and guardian of Dharma) and Vishnu, the destroyer

Mãyã is yet another interesting philosophical concept of illusion or "deception, having dual apparently contradictory aspects: one is ignorance that prevents one from realising Brahman and the other is that of knowledge which leads one to Brahm. However, this concept is inseparable from Brahm and forms the foundation of mind and matter. Besides Maya, the Upanishads also explain the unifying principles of the Universe in simple terms: power, breath, food, thereby uniting matter and spirit. As for the ranges of matter, certain zodiacal signs are characteristic of certain levels of matter. For instance: Caduceus, the symbol of god Mercury, is used to depict the process of Creation and Evolution in cycles. Similarly, the time-factor, the Limitation of the Infinite, is represented by Saturn, sometimes called Chromos, the god of Time. However, the planets Uranus and Neptune being the planets of collective unconscious and beyond time, they are not included in this series. Next in the list are Mars and Venus, in the order of their orbital distance from the sun. Mars is believed to 'govern the astral range', while

Venus essentially operates in the range in which objective thought operates. Next on the list is Mercury. This planet is astrologically associated with the Mind. In short, we have three factors: Spirit, Mind and Matter represented by Saturn, Jupiter and Mars — the Creative Trinity: Shiva-Vishnu-Brahma in Hindu philosophy corresponding to Christian Trinity: Father-Son-Holy Ghost

Puranas (ancient narratives) are important scriptures of Hinduism. So is Bhagavadgîtâ (The Song Celestial) of which monism is the essential theme, Mahabharata, Ramayana besides other mythological literature. Dharma, Karma, *Kundalini*, Meditation, Mysticism, Reincarnation, *Siddhis* and Universal force are some of the other essential elements of Hinduism. So is Samadhi, a particularly Hindu tradition amongst the saints. It is a significant experience of mystical ecstasy of which the foremost example in modern times is the experience of Sri Ramakrishna who describes his own first mystical ecstasy:

I was suffering from excruciating pain because I had not been blessed with a vision of Divine Mother. Life did not seem worth living. Then my eyes fell on the sword kept in the Mother's temple. Determined to put an end to my life, I jumped up and seized it, when suddenly the Mother revealed herself to me... The buildings ... the temple and all vanished, leaving no trace; instead there was a limitless infinite shining ocean of consciousness or spirit. As far as the eye could see, its billows were rushing at me from all sides ... I was panting for breath. I was caught in the billows and fell down senseless.

It was like dreamless sleep, a state in which the subject and object are dissolved into temporary union with Brahman. Hereafter the mere name of the Divine Mother could send Ramakrishna into Samadhi, a trance of ecstasy. It was like a sudden reprieve from death accompanied by a sense of overwhelming joy and gratitude. This phenomenon is best explained in the Brhad-ãryaka Upanisad:

As a man when in the embrace of his beloved wife knows nothing without or within, so the person when in the embrace of the intelligent self knows nothing within or without. That, verily, is his form in which his desire is fulfilled, in which the self is his desire, in which he is without desire, free from any sorrow. – IV.3.21:[1]

Ramakrishna experienced trances from an early age and became a priest at a new Kali Temple set up on the outskirts of Calcutta at Dakshineshwar in 1855 by a low caste widow Rani Rashmani. Ramakrishna did not know English or Sanskrit. Yet, he is revered for his varied and intense mystical experiences and his ability to express the same verbally as well as via his body language. This most famous and important modern Guru inspired the second most famous modern charismatic Hindu Guru, Swami Vivekananda who founded the Ramakrishna order of monks. He preached Vedanta to the West and India too, and introduced an element of social service in the new Order whose centers exist all over the globe.

Ramakrishna saw Kali everywhere. His mystical experience was writ large on his face, for everyone to see who met him. He was the living proof of higher states of consciousness and was referred to as the 'first incarnation of God who has been photographed'.[2] His child-bride with whom he never established sexual relations survived long after his transition to the 'Other Side'. She took on the divinity of her own as the Mother.

He was initiated into Advaita Vedanta and Tantra. In 1866 he was initiated into Islam by a Hindu Sufi and held that faith for three days during which he dressed like an Arab Muslim, said their prayers five times a day, and devoutly repeated the name of Allah several times a day. Hindu thinking completely disappeared from his mind for those three days during which he achieved full realisation of the sadahna (ritual practice) of the Islamic faith.

References

1. Radhakrishnan S.: The Principal Upanisãd, Harper-Collins, 1944; p. 262. Also as quoted by Collin Wilson in MYSTERIES, Watkins Publishing, London, 2006; p.35
2. David Smith:*Hinduism and Modernity;* Blackwell Publishing, Oxford, UK; pp. 162, 174

12

Psychic Applications

The lay public is generally inclined to believe that all this hoo-h? about spirits and the spirit-world, psychics, shamans and mediums undertaking fantastic journeys across to the "Other Side" and returning with wealth of information, are all mere figs of imagination. Well, may be so; may not be so; it is all a matter of one's personal belief-system. Come to think of it, who has seen the ?tm? or God, for that matter? It is your faith that shapes your mental attitude to these thought-processes.

Psychic energy has been put to positive use by those who are adept in the concerned field of knowledge and activity, or have received the gift of psychic ability from past life recall. Here we shall briefly examine some of these applications which have proved practically useful in everyday life.

PSYCHIC SURGERY

From the human angle this is perhaps the most beneficial application of psychic ability. One of the most famous psychic surgeons was a Brazilian named "Ze Arigo". Jose de Pedro, with education at the third grade level treated up to 300 patients a day and wrote medically correct prescriptions. And he did so for nearly two decades, correctly diagnosing every case and writing a correct prescription. He was reputed to be able to stop blood flow on a verbal command --- A gift from the gods, I suppose! Unfortunately, Arigo became a victim of bureaucratic archaic rules. He was convicted of illegal medical practice and sent to jail by the Brazilian Government in 1958 and again in 1964.

Paranormal surgery performed with bare hands and without the aid of surgical instruments and all the paraphernalia that goes with OT procedures, closing of the wounds again with bare hands, or surgery done with crude tools like kitchen knife, et al, fall in the field of psychic surgery. The patient remains fully conscious throughout the so called surgery and does not feel any pain either. The 'incisions' are closed without stitches and leave faint or no marks. Although surgery is performed under septic conditions, post operative complications like infections etc. do not occur either. This practice is largely prevalent in Philippines and Brazil --- at least it was so in the 1960's and 1970's when Spiritists used to be allowed to practice medicine.

The surgeon points a finger at the flesh, the patient feels a sort of tingling or jabbing sensation, a little blood may ooze out, which sometime turns out to be animal blood. Kidney stones have been found to be pebbles, tumors as chicken or pig organs, If the operation is a failure, the psychic surgeon would blame the spirits, or lack of harmony between the patient and the surgeon, or magnetic vibrations in the room.

One of the most famous psychic surgeons was a Brazilian named "Ze Arigo". Jose de Pedro, with education at the third grade level, treated up to 300 patients a day and wrote medically correct prescriptions. And he did so for nearly two decades, correctly diagnosing every case and writing a correct prescription. He was reputed to be able to stop blood flow on a verbal command— A gift from the gods, I suppose! Arigo was convicted of illegal medical practice and sent to jail by the Brazilian Government in 1958 and 1964.

In 1968 an American doctor Andrija (Henry K.) Puharich led a team of doctors to Brazil. ECG tests showed that Arigo did not have yogi-like ability to control his own blood flow, body temperature or brain waves. Nonetheless, Puharich concluded that Arigo controlled an unknown form of energy; Arigo had claimed that he was guided by the spirit of German "Doctor Fritz". Arigo was killed in an auto accident on January 11, 1971. The German doctor reappeared in 1980 as the spirit guide to a Brazilian obstetrician and gynecologist, Edson de Quieroz.

PSYCHIC READINGS

We in India rush to our Panditji, the Family astrologer, at the slightest provocation to seek advice on virtually any manner of family or financial problem, about the present or the future , or whatever. He (sometimes it is she) consults the charts for the stars configuration, and gives out his 'reading' as advice or prediction. The horoscope often comes handy. This process is more or less comparable to what has now come to be called 'psychic readings'. In the latter case a person uses his/her psychic ability to answer client's questions. The question and problems are no different from what we pose to our Panditji. This phenomenon has been in vogue since ancient times simply because an individual is always curious about the future. The consultation has now come to be called a "reading" that may last for about half to one hour or so. And if the "Panditji" happens to be a psychic it becomes a "psychic Reading". In the latter case the methodology varies between astrology and the so called Akashic Records with Numerology, Tarot, palmistry, psychometry, etc. filling the gap between the two ends of the spectrum.

Where and when the readings take place is called séances. Mediumistic séances are usually held in rather dark, dimly lit rooms with incense and candle lights on the sides. However, the latest development is in the field of mass readings conducted over the telephone, or even TV shows where the truth and reliability of the psychic is subjected to scrutiny besides of course answering the questions. The stories of psychic readings by mediums are innumerable, well documented and would fill volumes. It would therefore be more appropriate to concentrate on the world renowned most publicly tested psychic in history, the unbeatable George Anderson, for his conversations with the "Other Side" during which the spirits give him information about events that occurred during and after their own physical death, or that would occur in the future. George does not have a "Spirit Guide" like many other mediums do; he is like a radio-receiver through which the spirits communicate on a pre-ordained energy frequency to which only he is attuned to. His rate of accuracy varies between 86-95 per cent.

After a late night party celebrating their win David and Bret were walking home. A speeding truck struck them from behind. It was a 'hit and run' accident. David died and Bret was critically injured. Amongst other many friends, the coach of his soccer team came over to David's parents (Licatas) and gave them the very last shirt left in the locker room #27. He did not know that David had worn team shirt #27 on the Commack High School Varsity Soccer Team. Well, perhaps it could be sheer coincidence!

A friend of Barbara Licata told her that when her young daughter spoke to George at the radio station he said that a young boy was killed in a tragic accident. His soul was very restless from the tremendous sorrow and anguish that people were feeling. A coincidence of course! Barbara promptly called the radio station to get an appointment with George. She was firmly told not to give any details to the Station staff about herself, the family, and David, nothing whatsoever, not even her name. George must NOT know anything in advance about her circumstances, not even her last name. Barbara and her husband John announced their arrival at George's apartment. The constraints of space do not allow me to give the transcript of their interview; hence a summary only:

During the course of interview George continuously wrote automatically; that was his means of concentration. However, hid auto-writing and normal handwriting had nothing in common. He kept conveying whatever the spirits told him, getting affirmation from Barbara (but denial in an odd case). George told her that a young girl met him when he went over. She was with him now standing beside David. Must have died young, before David - Barbara confirmed that a young girl in their close neighborhood had been strangled about four months earlier and David knew her well. "David is very, very restless. Let's hope he can get it off his chest now ... He has to calm down, He is speaking so fast I can't even understand what he is saying." Barbara confirmed that David was a very sensitive and emotional person, and his was a strange case. Barbara confirmed that sixteen as a number meant something to her since David was 16 when he passed out. She confirmed that someone else, a male, was also involved and that David was struck on the head, and he was severely cut by the blow. Barbara denied that it was a cut by a bottle. George asked if David was murdered which she confirmed as an accident, but not deliberate murder. At this point George told David's spirit to calm down and tell him what exactly he wanted to. David came out with lot more, the crux of which was that he was not being vindictive, the murder was not intentional, he had met many of his relatives on the other side, that he was at peace and found the prayers from his Family very comforting.[1]

Barbara was deeply moved as was John. Their perception of death and attitude towards it were profoundly changed. Incidentally, George had very difficult times in his childhood and early adult life because of the visions and was diagnosed as a severe case of serious mental illness.

George was introduced to Joel Martin, Director of the psychic shows on radio/telephone or otherwise by Madeline, the production assistant for the shows. Martin was highly skeptical of mediums like George and did not believe that someone could communicate with the dead. He assured Madeline that he would expose George in a minute! Nonetheless, he met George and said that Madeline had told him that George received messages from the dead. George corrected him: "From those on the other side". George got some papers and pen for auto-writing and warned Martin to answer his questions only by indicating 'yes' or 'no' and offer no other information. George started the reading by asking if Martin understood the name 'Solomon'. Martin tried to put him off by saying 'Sol' but George persisted that he was being told 'Solomon', a father figure. Martin finally, reluctantly, admitted that George was right in that Solomon was his grandfather. George told Martin that he was seeing the Star of David over his head at which he looked up but saw none (!) which means your grandfather was a traditional Jew. The reading went on the same lines about Martin's sister, daughter, and so on. George had been accurate about everything. However, Martin wanted to test George still further. So he asked him to read an anonymous subject over that was about the maternal Aunt, then about another in the family, back to the Aunt on the other side, some very ill for whom the Aunt is waiting, then about a Brother. The Father of the subject and his Grandfather—all personal details were found correct. Last, but not the least, was the topic of subject's own health. George correctly diagnosed about the heart attack and subsequent complication of arteriosclerosis about which Martin, a close friend of the subject had no inkling whatsoever. George had proved beyond any doubt that he was all the time communicating with spirits of those on the other side: communicating with the dead.

When George was asked if we all go to the other side when we die, he answered 'yes' but preferred to call it 'making the transition'. He emphasised that we don't die, we merely shed our physical bodies and the soul makes a transition to the other side in a spiritual form. Death is a transition, not a terminus - Back to Bhagavad-Gita, the Song Celestial, 2:20. By now George had established credibility of his readings beyond question. Texts of his readings would fill volumes; any further elaboration does not merit consideration. However one aspect that is connected with psychic criminology is certainly worth noting.

In a group reading open session George saw the spirit of a beautiful woman standing close to a stranger. He asked the person if she was his wife. The man denied vehemently. But the woman's spirit accused the man of murdering her and George told him so. Where is she? She is standing next to you. Her name is Jean. There was terror in the eyes of the accused while all that George saw was the murder scene enacted by the spirit. George saw the woman being stabbed repeatedly, beaten and falling on the floor of the living room, her hands raised in a futile bid to save herself. George dare not say what he saw but the spirit kept repeating; he murdered me. When is someone going to do something about it?

The man was gone, just vanished. Information obtained via psychic means is inadmissible in a court of law.

Conscious self of the medium plays a major role in psychic readings. So it does in "Channeling" too. However in the phenomenon of channeling information is received by the medium from a source other than the conscious self. These sources are nonphysical beings like the spirits of the dead, angels, totem or guardian spirits, deities, demons, extra terrestrial beings and, last but not the least, the Higher Self. The process takes place in an altered state of consciousness. As a form of medium ship channeling has existed in most cultures since ancient times, in its modern avatar channeling has come to be associated exclusively with delivery of religious or spiritual messages allegedly emanating from highly evolved nonphysical entities. The ancient Indian seers, Buddhist high lamas, the Egyptian priests, Greeks, Chinese, Babylonians, Celts, et al, had their holy men and women who received divine guidance that took the form of channeling. The oracles, shamans and the mediums did not convey their personal opinions or forecasts; they were merely acting as the vocal chords, the mouth piece, of other nonphysical beings, form the 'other side". In any case those in trance stage do not have the benefit of their conscious selves.

In other words, communication with gods in trance is an exceptional ability. If it is not manifested in childhood channeling occurs during spiritual development. To cite case in point: Pat Bodegas, a resident of Connecticut started practicing Transcendental Meditation twice daily in 1972. She began to experience inner visions and was scared lest she might be suffering from hallucinations. She therefore resorted to therapy. Concurrently, she joined a spiritual group to understand what was happening to her. During the next about two years she kept resisting the inner visions some of the times while during others, she would resist them. After a while she perceived as being of golden light which identified himself as Emmanuel.

This perception came to her via clairvoyance, viz. clear-seeing. The field of perception thus extends beyond the normal three dimensions to include the fourth just discussed. While etheric vision is three dimensional, 'astral vision' is four-dimensional. The latter embraces time and space and enables tie subject to view an object both inside and outside at once. Both these visions carry magnification properties.

Kevin Ryerson joined a meditation group organised around the study of teachings of Edgar Cayce. Six months after he started meditating channeling began spontaneously. It took him another six months to learn how to control the visions, and the process of channeling. The entities that visited Kevin were many including an Essene[2] named John, an Irish pickpocket named McPherson as well as a West Indian, Obadiah by name. During her spiritual search Shirley MacLaine did a channeling session with Kevin. When she was filming the TV mini-series based on her book Out on a Limb, she created a channeling session in which Kevin not only played the role himself but so did his visionary entities as well.

CHANNELING

Channeling may be spontaneous or induced. When a subject falls into sudden trance state or lapse of consciousness: that mental state is spontaneous channeling. The subject has no control over the process. However, when the subject is under induced channeling, he is fully in control. This state of mind may be achieved via meditation, prayer, self-hypnosis, fasting, chanting, dancing, sleep-deprivation, breathing techniques, smoking herbs, or even taking hallucinating drugs; etc.

When the subject is in full trance his/her personality gets displaced and another entity or personality temporarily takes possession. At this point his voice and gestures undergo a change. He is unaware of what is said or done, and generally does not even remember what he said. Mental channeling may also be done under light trance conditions when the channeler remains fully or partially aware of the process.

A byproduct of phenomenon of channeling has been the encouragement it has imparted to individuals to develop their own connections to a higher wisdom, especially through intuition.

PSYCHIC ARCHAEOLOGY

Psychic Archeology was put to practical application, perhaps for the first time in 1907, when the Church of England appointed Frederick Bligh Bond for excavation of the ruins of Glastonbury Abbey in England to find the remains of two chapels. It was known that the two chapels once existed but were destroyed after Henry VIII closed all Roman Catholic monasteries following his break with the RC Church. The English Church was not aware that Bond was an occultist. He sought the services of his friend John Allen Bartlett, an auto-writer, and with him appealed to the spirits associated with the Abbey for help in locating the ruins of the chapels. An entity that identified himself as "Guillemots Monarchs", or "William the MONK" and other spirits who collectively identified themselves as the "Watchers from the Other Side" and the "Company of Glastonbury" provided all the detailed information regarding the Edgar and Loreto chapels along with the drawings of the buildings. The information was in Latin and Old English which the spirit said they had obtained from a "Universal Memory". They also said that Henry had brought about the downfall of the abbey out of his greed. They wanted the abbey to be restored to its old glory.

In the excavations Bond found everything exactly as the spirits had indicated. He kept his source a well kept secret until 1917 when he published his account in the Gate of Remembrance. The Church of England was very embarrassed over the disclosures and Bond became a persona non grata. He was removed from the assignment and excavations came to a stop in 1922.

The technique adopted by Bond involves clairvoyance other psychic skills, and its application to archeology has come to be known as Psychic Archeology. Taken in its broadest sense Psychic Archeology is employed virtually by all archeologists and anthropologists. It is therefore more of intuitive archeology that Bond was also using.

A byproduct of above was experiments in psychic Archeology by Polish scholars. They did so in the wake of success achieved by Chemical Engineer Stephen Ossowiecki in the 1930's. He had received training in Psychometry from a Jewish mystic. The experiments related to artifacts and he stated that the Magdalenian people existed about 15,000 years ago and were then using bows and arrows. But Stefan was killed by the Nazis before he could prove his point. However, later it was established that his conclusions were more than correct.

Stephen believed that his information came from the Akashic Records. Edgar Cayce has provided similar useful information for excavation sites in Egypt, the Sphinx, and the Great Pyramids. Similar techniques are being used to dig sites in North America and elsewhere. The Canadian archeologist J. Norman Emerson has worked with psychic George McMullen. The latter says that when he holds an artifact in his hands, he sees movie like images, a sort of slide-show while holding artifacts and claims that he is aided in his work by beings of light. To go a step further, McMullen Psychic Hella Hammid were taken to Egypt where they provided information about the buried city of Maria, the ruins of Marc Antony's palace and tomb, Cleopatra's palace etc. This team also located the ruins of an underwater temple beside the Lighthouse of Pharos in Alexandria.

Bishop Leonia's Polk told Professor James Rhodes Buchman, Dean of the Faculty at the Electrical Medical Institute in Covington, USA, that he could detect brass in the dark because its touch left a metallic taste in his mouth. It was rather mysterious how a metallic touch could affect the organs of taste! However, his experiments proved that this could. He wrapped various medicines in parcels and found that his students could detect the nature of medicines merely by holding the parcels in their hand. His success rate was astonishingly high. His conclusion: Nerves produce some sort of current or force which operates like an extra sense. He called it "nerve-aura". This led to his coining the word 'Psychometry', ability to discover information by the sense of touch alone. To carry the experiments a step further, the Professor asked a friend to write down his name on a sheet of paper and handed over the folded paper to a woman who was reputed for her remarkable talent at psychometry. She was able to describe the character of the man to an astonishing degree of accuracy. Professor Buchanan finally concluded that, when psycometrists hold objects belonging to a certain person, they can describe even intimate personal details of that person since all substances give off 'emanations' which are affected by human emotions.[3]

PSYCHIC ATTACKS

Paranormal assaults upon humans or animals that cause physical or mental distress, injury, illness, et al are classified as Psychic attacks. Even death could result from such attacks. In the field of sorcery such an attack is called a curse. In some tribal societies a 'curse' may cause a wasting disease that drains out blood from the victim's body so much so that he dies in the end. Such wasting diseases generally do not respond even to proper medical treatment. A snake or scorpion may be used for sending the curse, while in other cases a doll or a snip of victim's hair serves a sympathetic magical link that transmits the attack. Psychic attack is said to happen by the following means:

- Human direction such as a sorcerer;
- Non-physical agents like malevolent spirits, demons, or via a thought-force;
- A human assault by OBE projection by a 'double' or astral form.

The most common symptom of psychic attacks is the "hag syndrome" in which victim awakens feeling a crushing load on the chest, generally accompanied by paralysis. In some attacks the victim may hear strange noises, smell bad odors and may also suffer nightmares. "Hag Syndrome" has been documented since ancient times because sorcery and magic used to be the order of the day, and still is in remote tribal areas all over the world. It is estimated that hag syndrome presently occurs in 15 per cent of adult population worldwide. Modern theories attribute this to sleep disorders, indigestion, sexual repression, etc. However, folklore traditions continue to blame witchcraft and sorcery which, perhaps, is accepted as the general belief. Nonetheless, restless spirits of the dead ones cannot be ruled out.

Dion Fortune, the Occultist, in her monumental work on the subject (Psychic Self Defence-1930) says that such attacks are much more common than generally believed. She cites her own personal experience at age twenty when she was nearly psychologically destroyed by an employer whom she believed was adept in occultism. She suffered a nervous breakdown and believed her aura had depleted as if the battery had been drained. According to Ms. Fortune other symptoms of psychic attack include:

Philosopher William James recorded *(in The Varieties of Religious Experience- 1902)* a man's experience of a hag attack characterised by an invisible presence evoking a feeling of horror, a sensation of pressure on the chest, and "a large tearing vital pain." He further notes that for the attacks to be most effective, they are lunched during the waning moon, especially at the new moon.

Prescribed defences against psychic attacks are:

- To sever all contact with suspected people, places, paths of study;
- Avoid going to the sea/rivers since water is the element of psychic forces;
- Keep the stomach full since that shuts down psychic centers that serve as the port of entry;
- Get plenty of sunshine;
- Avoid being alone;
- If you are trained in occult practices, undertake certain protective/ banishing rituals;

As noted by Fortune Dion in her Psychic *Self Defence* published at York Beach in 1930.

PSYCHIC CRIMINOLOGY

Seeking help of seers and dowsers to locate missing persons, and to solve criminal problems, is as old as the history of society itself. However, the use of psychics in the investigation and jury selection of civil and criminal cases is not only of recent origin but is still considered a controversial issue. Nevertheless, it got a boost after World War II due to publicised success of some celebrity psychics, albeit the field of psychic criminology started taking shape in mid-19th Century when American physiologist, Joseph R. Buchanan coined the term 'psychometry'. He explained that the technique could be used to measure the 'soul' of all things. He further elaborated that the past is entombed in the present and objects retain imprints of the past and their owners whose 'vibrations' or 'psychic ether' or 'aura' could be picked up by sensitises.

Sir Arthur Conan Doyle, creator of Sherlock Holmes, predicted in 1925 that the detectives of the future would be clairvoyants, or would use clairvoyants. By the end of the 20th Century hundreds of such psychics were working with the police in North America, Britain and Europe, albeit not officially acknowledged as such. Moreover, their success rate, more often than not, was rather erratic. They generally worked pro bono and preferred to be classified as 'intuitive' to avoid a perceived taint on the term 'psychic'. However, they had no hesitation in accepting a fee from private parties to the case.

Most psychometric criminology involves handling of personal items of the victim, preferably under-clothing since they yield better 'vibrations', or objects directly from the crime-scene. By handling these objects the psychics claim they can perceive enactment of the crime, or at least get some images emanating from them, besides possibly the location of the body, murder-weapon, or the accused at best. Like the police, they do visit the crime scene to collect information specific to their calling.

Selection of juries is another field where psychic-abilities have been found useful. They also advise the attorneys when a witness is lying, or when a settlement offer may come through. If nothing else, the very presence of psychics helps in getting honest answers from jurors.

To cite a case in point: Defence lawyers for Jean Harris, convicted in the murder of Dr. Herbert Tarnower of New York were advised by a psychic that Harris would be convicted if she testified. The prediction proved true. However, testimony by psychics is not admissible in a court of law. Further, it raises the question of constitutional rights of privacy, particularly when a psychic picks up some threads from the mind of the suspect thereby violating the right to privacy. Of necessity therefore psychics have to work behind the scenes.

PSYCHOKINESIS (PK)

The most famous Soviet PK subject was Nina Kulagina, a housewife from Leningrad, born in mid-1920's, whose abilities were revealed to the West in 1968. Kulagina was observed by Western scientists, who witnessed such phenomena as the movement of many different sizes of stationary objects; the altering of the course of objects already in motion; and impressions on photographic film. Kulagina also exerted PK on a frog's heart that had been removed from the animal, first by changing its rate of beating and then stopping it altogether. She was also photographed levitating objects.

The case of New York based artist-psychic is another example of where the subject can influence an inanimate object. Ingo Swan could change the temperature of nearby static objects by one degree, besides affecting the magnetic field of a magnetometer— all through the power of PK.

Researchers have noticed a 'linger effect' in many experiments. For example, temperatures influenced by an agent continue to rise or fall for a period of time after the agent leaves the premises. Water has been held be healers and seems to influence the growth of plants continue to exert the influence even after being boiled. Plants too have souls, emotions and reactions. This notion must not be dismissed as unscientific, more so since it is consistent with the discoveries about the 'blueprint of life' supported by Kirlian photography.

In other words PK is the apparent influence of the mind over matter through invisible means. The term Psychokinesis comes from the Greek words 'psyche' (breath, life or soul) and 'kinetin' meaning motion. It occurs spontaneously and deliberately, indicating thereby that it is both unconscious and conscious process. The phenomenon has been known from ancient times in one form or the other --- levitation, miraculous healings, invisibility, luminosities, etc. that have been attributed to holy persons over the ages. The New Testament quotes many events resembling PSI and PK. However, what PK is and how it operates remains an enigma. All one can say is that it cannot be explained by any forces or laws of physics. It is an enigmatic supernatural ability bestowed on certain extraordinary individuals.

Magic spells, curses, rituals to control the weather, universal belief in 'evil eye', et al, are manifestations of PK. Man, ancient or modern, particularly amongst the tribal communities, have always believed in the existence of evil forces of nature, manipulated by masters of such forces. Belief in the existence of demons with an endless list of their names plays an important role in magical effects of evil forces. According to one version there are nine different varieties of demons. There are various methods by which the magicians invoke or dismiss these demonic powers.

Another medium renowned for PK was Rudy Schneider. His phenomenal expertise at telekinetic movement of objects was a subject of serious study in the first half of the 20th Century. American parapsychologist J.B. Rhine conducted an experiment with a gambler who used to claim that he had the power to influence the falling dice to turn to specific numbers, or combination thereof. Early results were certainly beyond the probability of chance. However, subsequent trials yielded uneven results. One thing was clear: subject scored well and accurately during the early parts of the experiments but his abilities deteriorated as the hours went by. Rhine also discovered that PK is not linked to any physical process of the brain. He was of the opinion that faith healing and folk magic healings were really PK phenomenon. However, he found PK had many similarities with ESP in some respects.

References

1. The foregoing summation and the others to follow are based on lengthy records of 'Readings' in WE DON'T DIE: George Anderson's Conversations with the Other Side by Joel Martin and Patricia Romanowski.
2. A member of a monastic brotherhood of Jews in Palestine from the 2nd Century B.C. to second Century A.D. was known as an Essene.
3. Collin Wilson: Op. Cit. p. 385.
4. Collins Wilson: The Psychic Detectives; San Francisco, 1985; Mysteries Watkins Publishing, London, 2006
5. Gulati M.N.: Enigmatic Tibet; Manas Publications, 2005, New Delhi.

13

Thanatology

(Death-bed Visions)

Thanatology is the scientific study of death. The study shows that death is not a terminus, but a mere transition. It is a rite of passage to be undertaken with dignity. Tibetan Book of the Dead deals with the art of dying at great length while the Western civilisation, till recently of course, and still does, take this passage to the Other Side with great fear and trepidation. It is all a question of the collective mind-set of the community and its culture. If a dying person has been spiritually prepared for death, as they do amongst Tibetans as well as many Indian and Asian communities, the person passes away in peaceful radiance looking forward to a peaceful happy life on the Other Side. However, the fundamental question remains: What is it that really dies?

A human body is made up of billions of cells. All of these cells die off every eight years. Since not a single atom of what a person was eight years ago is now alive in the body, it is not the same individual today that was eight years ago. This is the essential biological fact to remember. So what a person is today is not the same individual that was eight years ago! When a person's head is cutoff, every cell in the body continues to live as if nothing had happened. The hair and the nails continue to grow. In other words, it is some one or more of the 'higher selves' that really die.

The deathbed-visions are precursor of what is to come. These are paranormal experiences of the dying. The visions are apparitions of the dead and of an 'after world'. They bring peace and comfort to the dying person whose agony and distress suddenly disappear, or are mitigated via the mystical experience. In 1924 an obstetrical surgeon reported that when the last moment was approaching her patient transformed her into a state of peace and radiance just before she died. Of course these are subjective observations beyond scientific or clinical proof. Those who work with the terminally ill find this an everyday experience amongst their patients. Such patients share common characteristics that are not influenced by external factors such as racial, cultural, socioeconomic, religious, educational, age, etc.

The attendants of terminally ill often perceive a variety of beings of light, apparitions of the dead known to the dying, as if they have come to summon the patient to come over and join them. That is how many a dying person has reported the state of mind in those critical moments, may be incoherently at best. Unusual light and energy seem to pervade the room. Symbols of transition such as gates, bridges, rivers, boats are common forms of visions, sometimes accompanied by celestial music. Such symbolism is reported to last barely five minutes or so before the patient passes away to the Other Side. Statistically speaking, approximately 76 per cent of the patients died within ten minutes of the visions. A noteworthy point is that in most cases, the patients are fully conscious when the visions appear. The mystery of the phenomenon of multiple personalities— the complete transfer of personality from one body to another adds further complications. Professor Ian

Stevenson, an eminent parapsychologist of University of Virginia has studied the case of reincarnation of one three-and-a half-year-old Indian boy, Jasbir Lal Jat who died of smallpox but revived a few hours later with a totally new personality. The strange new personality identified himself as a man from another village who had died after eating sweets mixed with poison. He had detailed information about that man's life and family. He had died almost at the same time as the child went into 'death trance' thereby suggesting the complete transfer of personality from one body to another.[1] Professor Stevenson, as was his practice, was quite thorough in his investigations and confirmed that the boy was telling the truth. This is a parallel case with that of the two school girls of Ludhiana mentioned earlier.

References

1. Barrett Williams: Death-Bed Visions; *The Psychological Experience of Dying,* England 1926. Colin Wilson: op. cit. p. 38

14

Auras

Aura is there but there is no scientific evidence of its existence. All life forms emanate vital in varying degrees of intensity. Emanuel Swedenborg, the 18th century clairvoyant wrote in his Spiritual Diary: "there is a spiritual sphere surrounding every one, as well as a natural and corporal one." It is an envelope of vital energy, a halo of light, invisible to normal vision that appears to radiate from everything in nature: minerals, plants, animals and humans. It can be seen by those blessed with clairvoyance and occult powers when it may appear as a multicolored mist that fades off into boundless space throwing invisible sparks, rays and streamers. But please note that normal vision cannot see this spectacle; only the occult, the clairvoyant can perceive this colorful spectacle. This may sound as figs of imagination run wild; but then every one of us is not an occultist, or a clairvoyant, but does possess a magnetic field called bio-field. However, our magnetic field is not strong enough to produce a light emitting aura. Nevertheless, the possibility is that aura might be a form of light vibrating at much higher frequencies beyond the normal range of vision. A fitting analogy is the range of sounds that our pets can hear but we humans can't ...

Scientific research in the field of light rays has far advanced so much so that ultra violet rays can be made visible via rather crude and simple apparatus. In an experiment conducted by psychotherapists, clairvoyant test-subjects were seated in totally darkened rooms when they could "see" flame-like energy radiating from fingertips, animals, plants and magnets. The flames were described as red, orange, green and violet which alternately appeared and disappeared, and so on. Dr. Walter J. Kilner in-charge of electro-therapy in St. Thomas Hospital London discovered that an apparent human aura can be made visible through a specially designed apparatus. He divided the aura into three parts:

- The inner most layer is made of some fine material, a transparent dark space, narrow and often obliterated by the second band: the Professor labeled it as *'etheric-double'*;
- the inner aura, fairly constant in size and the densest portion;
- The outer aura, inconstant in size, which often appears blended into the inner aura.

He formulated a method of 'auric-diagnosis' of illness. He noted that weak and depleted auras suck off the auric energy of healthy persons. It seems that a person's physical health is related to the part of the aura that is closest to the body, the vital or etheric body as it is often called.

Clairvoyance healers say that illness first manifests itself first in the etheric body and the symptoms start appearing in the physical body at a much later stage. Edgar Cayce used to say that he saw colored fields around the people, which he learned indicated their state of mind, health and spiritual development. It will thus be seen that all this talk about human aura is, after all, not all that humbug! Some of the different bodies said to exist are:

- Etheric body: Penetrated by chakras or, or energy vortexes, which enable the universal life force to enter and nourish the organism. The seven major etheric chakras are: The root (*mûladharâ*); the sacral (svadhisthana), the solar plexus (*manipurna*); the heart (anahata); the throat (*visuddha*), the brow (*ajna*); and the crown (*sahasrara*);
- Astral body: also emotional, the seat of emotions and the vehicle for consciousness in OBE and NDE. It is said to be a non-solid duplicate of the physical body, and to have its seven primary chakras, which are separate from those of the etheric body.
- Mental body: The seat of intellect and thought;
- Casual body: The closest to the Higher Self.

SPIRITUAL BODY

The discovery of human electrical fields led to yet another line of treatment in medical practices, particularly those in the East. In fact both Chinese and Russians, and now many others in the western world, are deeply interested in the science of 'Acupuncture'. It is based on the assumption that lines of force crisscross the body and their junctions are the acupuncture points which control the health of the body. Cures are affected by inserting a needle at these points and vibrating it. This technique can also be used to produce anesthesia. Teams of Western TV channels have photographed serious life saving surgeries being carried out while the patient was conscious and smiling at the camera.

In order to ensure that the acupuncture points are located accurately, a device has been designed to measure their L-fields. The device measures skin resistance at the acupuncture points by moving an electrode on the surface of the skin. At the acupuncture point the electrical resistance suddenly drops which in turn lights up a bulb, pinpointing the acupuncture point.

References

1. Doyle, Sir Arthur Conan: *The History of Spiritualism*; Doran, New York, 1926.

15

Thought Forms

Thought is a powerful force. Every thought generates vibrations which, in turn, can create nonphysical entity as in the field of occultism. The nature and intensity of thought imparts floating form and colors to the nonphysical entity. These thought forms radiate out and attract sympathetic essences. Clairvoyants can visually perceive these thought forms, while others may sense them at intuitive level. All this may sound hocus-pocus to the non-believers. However, personal experiences of a French explorer, author and scholar of Tibet, the first western woman to enter Lhasa, the forbidden capital, Lady David-Neel Alexandra spent fourteen years in Tibet to unravel Tibetan mysticism and magic, may be partly only, prove beyond doubt the veracity of the phenomenon of nonphysical entities generated by Thought-Form is a reality and not mere figs of imagination.

David-Neel was born in Paris as Louise Eugenie, raised in Brussels, was introduced to occultism at age fifteen, spent quite some time in London from where she returned to Paris to study at Sorbonne. She inherited a substantial fortune in 1891 and travelled to Ceylon and India to the edge of the Himalayas to pursue her interests in Buddhism. After returning to Paris she worked as a singer when she met Philip Neel, a bachelor and engineer and became one of his mistresses around 1900. By then she was thirty-two and had termed herself as a "rational Buddhist' and wrote extensively on the subject. They got married four years later. It was a stormy marriage and she left but they remained married. She lectured in London and Paris to Theosophical audiences and returned to India in 1911 to study oriental languages. Philip Neel supported her financially for most of her subsequent travels and explorations.

In 1912 David-Neel met the Mharajkumar (Crown Prince) of Sikkim, Sidkeong Tulku who invited her to Gangtok, near the border between India and Tibet. Notwithstanding the age difference (the Prince was much younger) the two developed a romantic friendship. David-Neel was totally enchanted by Tibetan culture and customs. The Prince introduced her to the Lamas of both the Red Hat (Traditional) and Yellow Hat (Reformed) branches of Buddhism.

David-Neel met the Thirteenth Dalai Lama at Kalimpong. She had two audiences with His Holiness, the first on April 15, 1912. After the second, a naljorpa (a wizard) advised her to travel to Tibet which, of course, was otherwise forbidden to all foreigners. She therefore returned to Sikkim to resume her studies in Sanskrit wherein she believed her future lay for pursuing her Buddhist research-studies. The Crown Prince died in 1914 cutting her off the royalty, and she could not return to Europe because of the World War. She decided to become a disciple of Gomchen (Great Hermit) who lived as a hermit at De-Chen in a cave of Clear Light at an altitude of 12,000 ft. The Gomchen agreed to instruct her in Tibetan and Tantra in exchange for complete obedience and to teach him English. So she took up residence in a cave about a mile below that of the *Gomchen* who gave her the name "Lamp of Wisdom". A minor *tulku*, aged about fifteen named Aphur Yongden, was assigned to her as a servant. Later she adopted him as her son and he became a lama in his own right in course of time.

As David-Neel progressed in her studies under Gomchen she developed a telepathic rapport with him, the highest form of psychic development a student can look forward to. Besides this, Gomchen also taught her the art of *tumo* breathing by virtue of which Tibetan yogis can keep themselves warm and comfortable under frigid winter conditions. This breathing-system also goes a long way in preparing the yogis for spiritual emancipation. She also leant the art of lung-gom traveling, a type of entranced movement in which a body moves very fast without rest, food or water. Lung-gom-pas bounce along as if their bodies are extremely light weight; may be at times they almost fly through! For some reason, perhaps of previous life experiences, David-Neel felt that she belonged to Central Asia and did enter Tibet in 1916, illegally of course, but not hat illegally since the Panchen Lama, second in rank only to the Dalai Lama, had invited her to his monastery at Shigatse. Since the British treated Tibet as their sort of protectorate, they expelled her from her Sikkim hermitage. Consequently, all her servants and entourage deserted her except Aphur Yongden who held a British passport. The two thereafter left for Japan and from there, surreptitiously, for Tibet on yet another dangerous journey with the honorable goal of making it to Kumbum Monastery. She spent nearly two-and-a-half years in Kumbum where she translated a number of rare Tibetan manuscripts into French and English besides observing psychic and magical feats if Tibetan adepts.

Yet another dangerous inordinately long journey from Kumbum to Lhasa, the dream city for every Tibetan and adventurer, lasting nearly three years was in store for David-Neel. No hotels-motels on the way! She had to take recourse to tumo-breathing to stay warm in snowy caves, but she could not take recourse to lung-gom as that would easily separate her from her companions. It was 1921, and she had no money; perhaps the Chinese officials had stolen the remittance from Philip back home. She was in tatters and often the victim of bandits; but they never harmed her. However, the last part of the journey was through exceedingly dangerous Po country whose inhabitants were reported to be cannibals. On the contrary they often offered her hospitality. Yongden passed her off as the widow of a sorcerer to cajole offerings from the rustic peasants. Sometimes she masqueraded as a Kamdora, a female spirit whose blessings are usually sought by the gullible.

Reaching her goal Lhasa in February 1924 proved to be an anticlimax as stated by her in her account of the trip, *My Journey to Lhasa* (Boston, 1986). With her tattered costumes and disheveled appearance she could possibly not derive any benefit from the educational and spiritual facilities available in that sacred City. Now she was anxious to leave. By 1925 she and Yongden were back in Paris. After all! Three years later she purchased a small villa in southern France and named it "Samten Dzong", the "Fortress of Meditation". After Philip's death in 1941 she acknowledged having participated in and observed Tantric sexual rites during her travels, besides other escapades.

Before closing this part of the story and reverting to thought-forms, I might as well allude to Chöd (to cut up) ritual, a grim otherwise revolting sort of ceremony symbolic of Buddhist concept of impermanence. It is designed to harness occult forces and liberate the subject from all attachments. In this rite the subject sacrifices his (her) body by dismemberment and offering the remains to hungry horde of ghouls for them to devour the same.

David-Neel's works include more than thirty titles. She passed on to the *other-side* in 1969 at age 101. During her lifetime she received numerous honors and awards most prominent of which were the French Legion of Honor, the Gold Medal of the Geographical Society of Paris, and the Insignia of the Chinese Order of the Brilliant Star. It goes without saying that reasons for the British Royal Geographical Society not to bestow any honors are much too transparent to students of history of British Indian Empire.

Thought-forms fall into three classes:[1]

- The image of the Thinker: (Bilocation);
- An image of a material object associated with the thought;
- An independent image expressing the inherent qualities of a Thought.

Negative thoughts like lust, greed, anger, hatred etc. produce thought-forms that are dense in color and form. On the other hand positive thoughts are light in form and color while spiritual thoughts generate forms that have greater purity, clarity, and refinement. The last mentioned ones are transparent in their intrinsic nature.

Thought-forms can be directed at an individual. However, if the receiver is not on the same mental frequency as the sender, the same can also bounce back on the sender. If you have hatred for a person but he does not hate you, then sending an evil thought-form to that person might prove equally damaging to you. Take care before you act on an evil intention. Good pure thought-forms naturally return purity and well-being. Nonetheless, just forming a thought is not enough. For a thought-form— good, bad or indifferent—to be effective and travel the desired distance, it is essential that it is strong, intense and clear enough. The characteristics of the original thought-form are of primary importance.

The same holds good for magical thoughts too. Tibetan mysticism describes two levels of generations of shadowy body. Their scriptures mention that an expert mystic who lives in a subtle body is called a "tulp?". They can also generate tulp?s from other living beings too. Sometimes a tulp? could be powerful enough to produce tulp?s for itself. The first generation of these clones or slaves is called "Yang Tula" and the next refinement is "Naing Tula". In other words a tulp? could produce a family of his clones! Only masters of this occult science can achieve such high rate of success and can manipulate their invisible but perceivable ageless subtle beings. They can do so through their t?ntric s?dhn?s, dreadful practices of forcefully separating the subtle from the physical - risky and explosive in nature. All that matters is our awareness that the Divine has endowed us with enormous power in the subliminal core of our Mind, which must never be misused in any way whatsoever.

By way of digression— I might as well narrate the story of Colonel Alcott and Madam Blavatsky, the then President of the Theosophical Society, were driving on the outskirts of Bombay. They saw a majestic Ashram on the roadside. While the Madam asked the Colonel to wait, she went inside the Ashram and after sometime came back with a bunch of garlands one of which she gave to the Colonel. Since the Colonel was enthralled by the majestic sight of the Ashram he went that side again the next day. But there was no sign of the Ashram; they could see only a lawn with some gardeners working on it. All enquiries about the majestic Ashram proved futile. Even the driver who had brought them there the day before confirmed that he had not seen any such Ashram anywhere around even yesterday! Later, the Madame explained the implications of a gross and subtle spiritually endowed Ashram of that nature. The 'existence' of gross and subtle siddha ashrams in deep

Himalayas as narrated by a revered saint of Bengal, Shriram Thakur further reinforces the concept in as much as these places remain non-existent for most people whose inner minds are dumb and dormant.

TULPA: An Imaginary Being

Tulpa is a Tibetan term which means an Imaginary being, created simply through the process of Thought-Concentration. In fact it is a thought form, albeit humanoid in appearance. When a crowd of demonstrators is fighting for a common cause for the common good, thought-forms occur spontaneously, simply because the 'group mind" is concentrating on the same objective. The demonstrators act in unison without being so directed by an outside agency. Same thoughts, goals and ideas all lead to unity of action. It is almost automatic. In other words, the "group mind" takes possession of the group. And when the group disperses, sodoes the *tulpa*, a life like chubby phantom.

Creation of thought-forms is one of the most puzzling enigmas of Tibetan spiritual-occult environment. They are really creatures of deep thought and imagination. Concentration-meditation is the essential pre-requisites for the mind to be able to create a tulpa which is generally a human, but could well be an animal or any mythical creature. Will power, visualisation and life-energy are essential ingredients that go to form a tulpa, consciously or even unconsciously. All living beings have life-energy, weak in some and strong in others.

Tibetans are not the only ones who believe in the existence of life-energy. The belief is widespread in many Central Asians, South and South Asian cultures besides Australian aboriginals, Amerindians. Amongst the latter, the Cherokees particularly believe that the spiritual energy is capable of creating thought-forms. However, the Tibetans are more specific on the subject. They believe in the human ability to actualise thought into physical entity through high concentration and mental focus on the objective so that the spiritual or invisible can manage to manifest itself in a physical form that can be perceived not only by the subject but by others also. However, contrary to Tibetan belief system, tulpas are not ghosts or apparitions; they are neither. In fact, ghosts are spirits of the dead while apparitions are shadows of the dead which appear at psychic séances. Instead, they are mere thought-forms only.

In the Western occult system, egregious are more or less equivalent to tulpas. Both can be captured on digital films. Both types have the ability to detach themselves from the control of their spiritual master, their creator, and transform into mischievous troublesome beings. For all practical purposes tulpas are mere psychic phantoms, at best to be avoided, and at worst to be dissolved. Incidentally, tulpas cannot converse. They are spiritual creatures of the highest order. Nonetheless, in all recorded cases tulpas have betrayed the person who willed them, and therefore had to be eliminated, often after considerable efforts, as it happenedwith David-Neel Alexandra. In fact, some tulpas become so rebellious that they fight the magician in all seriousness, and may even kill the latter.

In a number of cases tulpas have been sent on a mission, but do not come back. Instead, they roam around all over the place posing danger to the public at large. Sometimes the maker of the tulpa dies leaving the phantom behind. In that eventuality the phantom generally dissolves itself or gradually vanishes like a body that perishes for want of food. On the other hand, "some tulpas are expressly intended to survive their creator and are specially formed for that purpose". In order to verify the veracity of live thought-forms, David-Neel Alexandra decided to experiment on herself.

Instead of adopting the lamas' deities she chose a rather insignificant short fat chubby monk, innocent and jolly type, for her experiment. She went into isolation for concentration of thought and to perform other rites. The tulpa was formed as a phantom Monk. He became a kind of guest living in her apartment. At this point of time she broke her seclusion.

"Though I lived in the open, riding on horseback for miles each day, the illusion persisted.... The phantom performed various actions of the kind that are natural to travelers and that I had not commanded.... I felt as if a robe was lightly rubbing against me, and once a hand seemed to touch my shoulder... The fat, chubby-cheeked fellow grew leaner, his face assumed a vaguely mocking, sly, malignant look. He became more troublesome and bold. In short, he escaped my control. Once, a herdsman who brought me a present of butter saw the tulpa in my tent and took it for a living lama.... The presence of that unwanted companion began to prove trying to my nerves; it turned into a 'day-nightmare'. So I decided to dissolve the phantom. I succeeded, but only after six months of hard struggle. My mind-creature was tenacious of life. There is nothing strange in the fact that I may have created my own hallucination. The interesting point is that in these cases of thought-materialisation, others can also see the created thought-forms."

Such phantoms usually assume a human form and can be sent on a mission. David-Neel created her tulpa as a short, fat, jolly good fellow-monk. Initially he was really good, part of the apartment as a guest. But soon he became lean and thin, and started acting independently. He had his own independent mind and got out of control. Try as she may, her tulpa, the phantom, would follow her wherever and whenever. He became so obnoxious as to touch her and rub against her. Others could also see him too. The situation became so intolerable that she decided to eliminate the tulpa.

According to certain Tibetan rituals a tulpa can be dissolved. She tried again and again but the obstinate disobedient phantom resisted all her efforts. It took her nearly six months of hard work to eliminate the phantom. One theory explains this phenomena arising spontaneously out of the collective unconscious as archetypes which take on phantom or seemingly real form. This may perhaps explain the phenomena of devils, supernatural monsters, and possibly UFOs too!

The Concept of *Yiddam*

In a way, *Yiddam* is a corollary of tulpa. Yiddam is a divine teacher. Tibetans have a special regard for yiddam since it possesses an aspect of the enlightened mind. There are four main types: peaceful, powerful, wrathful and increasing. Whatever type it may be, it is essentially a risky proposition, like Alexandra's tulpa turned out to be. Ultimately it is for the student to decide what is best for him. However, the Guru generally recommends the 'powerful' type since that is likely to serve for a lifetime.

In order to evoke a Yiddam the magician studies images of a fearsome looking deity, more of a demon than a god. The study is serious, prolonged and profound. Even the smallest detail is examined in depth. The prospective student makes copious notes of all that transpires. Next, he is required to find a suitable site for evocation, preferably a well secluded cave on a mountain side. He is then instructed about the art of constructing a *kylkhor* (a magic circle), a very complex symbolic diagram more like the Hindu *Mandala* that is supposed to hold the yiddam, and not the magician. After the yiddam is evoked it is required to remain inside the magic circle leaving the magician alone outside. The mandalic kylkhor is made using the unique Tibetan art of sand-painting which might take months to complete. A Mandala may be constructed in any size but the traditional proportions must be maintained in all cases.

Tibetan sand painting uses six primary colors: white, black, blue, red, yellow, and green, four of the lat colors come in three shades of dark, medium and light. The sand is sprinkled using a narrow tube. Some teachers are such experts that they can manage to squirt out a single grain of sand in order to maintain the correct balance. The thin lines of a *mandalic kylkhor* could be as fine as the width of a single or two grains of sand! The student having learnt this technique retires to his chosen abode where he may have to work all by himself for months together. After the task of constructing the kylkhor is accomplished, the Yiddam must be persuaded to come out to accompany the student to enter the kylkhor. The student need not have any fear of the Yiddam since the Yiddam is an elaborate construction of his own mind.

"All and everything, without exception, is the product of the pupil's mind. This is the great secret of Tibetan occultism: the realisation that the world — all of the world without exception — is a mental construct. It has no existence outside of the mind that made it. For the mystic this great Truth is the key to liberation from the eternal wheel of birth, death and rebirth — why return to a world that does not really exist?"

References

1. Gurney Edmund: *Phantasms of the Living;* London, 1886.
2. Brennan J.H.: Occult Tibet; op. cit. p. 126.

16

A Search for the Truth

Ruth Montgomery was a journalist of repute, a syndicated Washington based correspondent on political and world affairs. She happened to go to an unplanned séance, the first ever she attended.[36] Her sister accompanied her. The medium, Dr. Pantin asked them to write any questions, which Ruth did. The question and answers ran into many pages. Suffice is to say that without any prior knowledge of the family or any personal details, the medium who by now called himself under the name of a spirit called 'Pedro', gave out all the answers, again running into a number of pages, accurately to the last detail. The skeptic in Ruth started mellowing, all the more so since Pedro had not, and could not have, read the questions since a black strip of cloth had been tightly tied over his eyes. Towards the end of the session a soft beating of drums started swelling into a deafening cacophony when an extremely loud voice bellowed that he was the 'Big Chief White Mountain', claiming to be "Ruth's Personal Protector"[37].

Ruth's next brush with spiritualist clan was at a 'materialisation séance' with Rev. Bertha Eckroad. The members were instructed to come forward, when called, and converse with the spirit-relative from the 'other side' but must not cross the '*laksman rekha*' towards the spirit as that would interrupt its 'ecto-plasmic connection leading to serious harm to Miss Bertha. The audience started singing hymns. Soon a diaphanously clad figure emerged from the cabinet, introduced herself as Bright Star and announced her mission was to help the departed relatives to appear through the medium's ectoplasm. When Ruth's name was called she went over and was told that her Grandmother Judy wished to speak to her. She had died at age eighty-three and was draped in milky whites, with long black hair flowing down her which she still retained. Her grandmother brushed Ruth's bare arm with her gossamer material that hung from her arms. As the parade of spirit-relatives continued, it was announced that Aseneth wished to greet Ruth and her husband together. She was dressed like all others before her but her facial features and hair coloring was distinctly different. She spoke softly of her pleasant life on the other plane. She said she recognised the hymn they had just been singing and disappeared after which singing was resumed in which Aseneth joined from behind the cabinet indicating that she remembered the family songfests.

Ruth and her husband Bob were indeed in exceptional luck that evening. They were summoned again to greet Bob's other sister, a former school teacher. She talked about her teaching duties on the other plane. When she started to say good-bye, Ruth claims that she picked up the courage and boldly asked her if she kiss Ruth. "Of course" and she did. Her hand touched Ruth, perhaps inadvertently (!) and Ruth, the skeptic, found the touch was surprisingly human. Next she kissed at Bob, but did not touch him before departing through the parted draperies of the cabinet.

Ruth had gone over to meet her friend Gladys who hobbled on her cast to a nearby chair and told her that she had just received some automatic writing that said, “Ruth will be able to do that now.” Then Ruth showed Gladys what she too had received just before leaving her house. It was the same — the circles and figure-eight are the spirits' way of expressing joy that at last they are able to establish contact with the right person. As Ruth sat down at Gladys's table and held a pencil in her hand, words started forming and gradually filled a full page without any effort or conscious understanding on Ruth's part. For Ruth, this experience was unbelievable. However, Gladys advised her not to spend more than twenty minutes or so on this activity, since they all in this world had their own lives to live, and could not live in two worlds simultaneously.

One day Ruth wrote, auto of course, that she must find a different house — an older type, with big rooms and high ceilings. The spirit told Ruth that the house should be beautiful, look charming, have a little garden patio, and be near George Town area. “You would find this house in R Street near the Library. Do not offer more than seventy thousand dollars. ... Go at once and buy it. We will take care of the rest.” After a series of errors in address of the proposed house, its location, date of ads etc., Ruth finally got all OK from her Guide except that the price demanded was far higher. Ruth got the message through auto-writing that the price would be brought down. “You must buy it. It is the one for you, and it has what we need for our project. ... Tell them you will pay seventy thousand dollars, but no more. ...”

The house was quite inconvenient. The stairwell was a big trouble, not for the discarnate spirits but certainly for Ruth and her family and domestic staff in human form. Ruth tried to persuade the spirits but Lily, the symbolic Guide, wrote via the fast moving pencil: “I must insist that you buy it. It was meant to be your home. It may be inconvenient, but it is the way you were meant to live. There is no way to avoid it. ... This is your destiny. Now, go to see it again. Make your offer and let us get on with our work." The arguments between the Guides and Ruth continued for some days, all via auto-writing of course. One day without the familiar sign of Lily, the pencil wrote: "Ruth, this is Dad. I want you to do what the Guide says. He knows what is best for you. ... You are one of the fortunate ones chosen for this work, and it is very necessary that you obey. ... It is a wonderful thing that lies ahead for you if you will do as bidden. This is all now. Ira." At the urgings of the pencil Ruth took Bob to the house again. When Ruth asked for identity of the Guide, the pencil wrote: "I was a writer of great note. I cannot tell you more at this time."

After a break of few days the pencil wrote: "This is the day you will get the house. It is for you and Bob, and our work. This beautiful house was made long ago for this purpose. Now relax. We will take care of the rest, including the sale of your house." Ruth signed the sale-purchase agreement and acquired the house which made the Guides happy to no end, expressed via the pencil. Two days later the pencil wrote: "Your house will sell this week for seventy-five thousand dollars. Now relax, smile and prepare for the week ahead." Next day an out-of-town friend called and told Ruth they were out to find a furnished house. The deal was struck within the predicted week. A month later, Ruth and family moved to the house on Sheridan Circle. QED!

References

1. Séance is a meeting in a windowless darkish room.
2. Most spiritualists in America believe that each one of them has an Ameri-Indian as a "spirit" bodyguard.

17

Ghosts and Apparitions

Ghosts are real. Yes, so real that you can feel their presence, see them and speak to them and also get a response from them mostly as a gesture, or even an audio response which may be rather rare. You can order a ghost to leave the place. They can go out of the house through the walls or closed doors also. You may order the ghost(s) to go to the 'light' via the 'tunnel', the course all souls follow to go to the "other side". No, I am not kidding nor trying to scare you, nor it is a fig of imagination. However, it is not within the power of every one to perceive the ghosts and communicate with them. Occult power, psychic ability, is the crux.

Of course, everyone is afraid of ghosts. The very thought or idea of presence of a ghost gives shudders to most people. But it is the fear of unknown that is the root cause of the problem. However, the fear is mostly irrational if only we could understand what a ghost is, its form and nature and what it is made of.

But the million dollar question remains: What is a ghost? What makes it, how and why?

Ghost is a soul gone astray. Soul is a form of celestial energy, like a blob or streak of energy, a piece of it so to say, with a chemical imprint on it. That is the recorded history of its past lives and what is the likely course of consequences of those karmas. Above all, ghost is transparent even though, at times, it may be shrouded in thick fog-like envelop.

Ghost is a colloquial word, rather crude. In fact, ghosts are apparitions of the dead — humans, spirits, animals or even inanimate objects. They are supernatural manifestations of the living.

Death is not a terminus; it is merely a transition from one form of life to another, to the "other side" where the essential element of life, the soul continues to lead perhaps a happier and more peaceful life, awaiting its turn for rebirth. For all practical purposes all souls go on to the other side, and they are called spirits. Some souls, for one reason or the other, continue to remain earthbound. They turn into ghosts and the place where they decide to live is said to be haunted, mostly the house in which the death took place, or where the person during his life time was emotionally attached, and from where he could not detach himself despite the body having perished. An intense desire for revenge for a major wrong, like murder, is often the cause célèbre for a soul to remain earthbound. They are afraid to face God because of their bad deeds. Some of them do not wish to meet their ex spouse on the other side so they remain earthbound while some ghosts do not believe that they are dead.

An unfulfilled romantic love could also be the cause célèbre for the soul to stay on looking forward to fulfillment of the desire. In all such cases the soul continues to inhabit the site of murder or the place of the loved one, inside it or hovering around it, coming in whenever it suits the apparition. They are the diehards who want to do things their own way. Be that as it may, it won't be correct to say that apparitions are mere mental hallucinations, or telepathic experiences. Ghosts-Apparitions are a reality and parapsychologists have provided enough evidence in this regard.

Most apparitions exhibit one or more of the common features like voices, noise, extreme cold, unusual smell, displacement of objects, use/misuse of facilities like beds and furniture, throw things hither and thither, etc. Presence of most apparitions is only felt and visual images are much less common. Apparitions may be corporeal, luminous or transparent and without proper shape. In order that they can be easily recognised, apparitions often appear in period-costumes, cast shadows, or get reflected in mirrors.

Apparitions generally make an appearance for some specific reason. To that extent they are different from what are commonly known as ghosts. They may manifest to communicate a possible death in the family, give advance warning of a looming danger or crisis, comfort the grieving, and so on and so forth. Apparitions also appear in battle zones. The spirits and ghosts are both souls. However, the main difference between the two is that while the spirit may visit our side but will return to the Home after the object of visit is achieved while a ghost is a soul that is earthbound for whatever reason.

From the foregoing we may classify apparitions as follows:

- Crisis Apparitions;
- Guardian Spirits;
- Grieving Spirits;
- Informative Spirits;
- Collective Apparitions;
- Reciprocal Apparitions;
- Deathbed Apparitions;
- Reincarnating Spirits.

During modern times acknowledgement of Para-psychological experiences is no longer considered weird. In fact, in polls conducted in the United States in the 198o's showed that 42 per cent of adult populations and 67 per cent of widows acknowledged paranormal experiences.

Ghost-Busters

Geography and cultural variations apart, ghosts are known to exist in all parts of the globe. If one has a haunted house there is every possibility that he/she would try and find someone who can provide succor by getting rid of the ghost(s). Naturally there is abundance of stories about ghost busters. Tracy Cochran's *The Real Ghost Busters*, Peter Underwoods' *The Ghost Hunter's Guide*, etc.; But the ones I have liked most are those narrated by Echo L. Bodine, primarily because she is also a good psychic medium and led a good team. One could fill volumes with all such stories, but that doesn't take us anywhere. So here I shall confine myself to a few ghost stories culled from Echo's book, *Relax, it's only a GHOST!*

The family had just finished dinner when the young man went down to the basement to practice on his drums. He was in the early learning stage and was therefore rather rough. A few moments later conversation around the dinner table came to a sudden end when music from the basement sounded as if a pro was playing at the drums. The family thought that it was a record (a tape) that he was playing. A few minutes later the brother dashed up the stairs, hysterical, pale and barely coherent. He asked if the family had heard him. "Yes, we did hear the excellent music. It was a good record". He denied and instead went on to explain that he was practicing as usual when a white figure floated through the closed door. That scared the h. out of him and he closed his eyes tight. But he could still see the white figure that was holding his hands and was basically playing the drums through his hands, making the really beautiful music.

The mother took the young man to a medium who said she was expecting the visit. It was the young man's "guardian angel" who had visited their house and played on the drums. The medium went on to say that all members of the family had some degree of psychic ability, the young man and his sister were particularly so gifted by nature. However, the Sister, Echo Bodine, had exceptional psychic ability and would make a mark in the field of medium-ship, particularly in dealing with spirits from the other side, and ghosts.

The following story in Eco's own words shows how gifted she was, psychically:

"My parents had gone away for the weekend, and this guy I was dating stopped by. He had been drinking and was coming on to me very aggressively. I felt afraid ... I silently asked my spirits in the house to do something ... the broom closet door opened all by itself. Out of the closet came the broom, floating good three feet off the ground. It moved through the entire length of the room we were in, then returned to the closet and fell on the floor. My intoxicated friend was out of there faster than you could say "poltergeist"!

The spiritual guides assist the psychic mediums to send the erring souls to the other side. The medium convinces the ghost(s) to go on to the other side after loud lengthy sermon-like speech-arguments. The ghost is then directed to float to the tunnel, go through it towards the Light, encouraging it all the way to the Light. This done, the medium burns sage[33]to clear the place of any negative energy that may have been left behind by the ghost(s). Generally speaking, there is more than one ghost in a haunted house; sometimes they come in flocks.

A ghost is not necessarily a powerful being. It comes close to you, face to face, and takes in your breath. By this it gains energy and power. They also gain energy from your fears. If you are in a group, they derive energy from fears of entire group and thus gain immense energy. Don't be afraid of ghosts: That's the principle. All ghosts are not mean, nor are they all troublesome. Most are OK; it is only a few who cause problems. That is because they had a difficult death or were murdered, tortured etc., and are now looking for revenge. Some ghosts were alcoholic in their lifetime. They are likely to take possession of a living addict and derive pleasure from the latter's alcoholic consumption! Some people in haunted houses like their ghost and treat them as their pets. In turn the ghost likes to be loved and treated as a pet. Such houses may not need services of a ghost buster.

As mentioned in the earlier story, there are many indications that a house is haunted. The most interesting one is: A house has been put on sale but it has not been sold despite repeated efforts by many realtors. Three such cases have been recorded by 'Echo'. In each case the ghost had his personal reasons why he did not want the house to be sold away. In one; the original builder liked the present tenants and did not want a change of occupancy; in another the ghost wanted the entire house to himself and in the third, the ghost was in love with the owner, a lady, and did not want the relationship to be disturbed. The ghost-busters team led by Echo succeeded in getting the ghost to move on to the other side thus redeeming the three distressed souls besides getting the house sold off within one week.

A member of church youth group requested Echo to check out his attic from which strange noises kept coming. The entire youth group accompanied Echo to the attic. They sat in a circle on the floor, held hands and switched off the only light overhead, waiting for something to happen. Soon Echo saw a small figure, a girl standing beside the boxes in the attic. Shortly, form of a woman appeared beside her. Both were holding hands and floating towards the circle. Suddenly a man in black came from the left. The woman and the little girl got frightened and darted back behind the boxes. Then he lunged towards the group. Seems everyone saw him. Echo reminded the group to say the Lord's Prayer and not to show fear. Too late! The man in black was getting bigger and bigger feeding on the energy he derived from fear of those in the group. He became about 12 feet tall. As we said the Lord's Prayer his size would shrink, and then would return to original.

Finally Echo picked up courage and yelled at him to leave the group alone. He laughed but disappeared. He did this several times while Echo shouted at him every time that he was not welcome to the house and must leave for good. Amazingly, whenever the man disappeared the woman and the child would come out from behind the boxes. While Echo was focused on the mother and child the tall man in black was on top of Echo. She yelled at him that he was not welcome at the house and to leave NOW, and not to come back. He went away. There was a small puddle of liquid on the floor at the center of the circle. Unexplained liquid! Echo waited for five minutes and concluded from the calm situation that the man was gone. As the group was preparing to leave, the little girl and her mother appeared again to thank Echo for getting rid of the man who had murdered them both, and then they too left. After this incident Echo left her full time job to devote to psychic practice. She and her brother appeared on radio-TV talk shows to do mass readings, go ghost hunting as and when, and sent numerous stray souls to the other side. Whenever the ghosts were in a group with some children around, she told the child-ghosts to hold hands of adult ghosts and walk together through the tunnel to the Light and not to let go till they were on the other side.

There are many such stories about Echo and her psychic brother. They became famous ghost-busters; but I shall call it a day here in so far as Echo and her brother are concerned. A house called Castel Mare in Middle Warberry Road, Torquay, was known to be haunted by the ghost of an insane doctor who had murdered his wife and maidservant on the premises. In late 1920's three young men decided to investigate the haunted house. The trio went to the place and found the atmosphere rather oppressive but certainly not frightening. One of them went up the stairs and stood alone in the upper hall waiting for his companions to join him. All of a sudden he felt the sensation as if his thoughts were going in slow motion while a black film seemed to cover the left side of his brain as if he was being anaesthetised. After great effort he managed to stagger outside and there he fainted. He felt low and tired when his brother in the team joined him. Meanwhile, the third member of the team continued alone with exploration of the house. Every few seconds he would whistle to indicate that all was well. Then the whistling ceased. The other two companions, the two brothers, immediately concluded that something was amiss and rushed to the scene where they found the third member of the team in a completely disheveled condition coated with dust and plaster. There was a serious physical struggle between him and a patch of greyish light which rushed past him, knocking him down; and it just vanished.

References

1. Sage is a mint, *Salvia officinalis*, having grayish green aromatic leaves.

18

Hello From Heaven

Our loved ones have not died. They are very much there on the "other side", keeping a watch over us, warning us from time to time of impending danger, protecting us, and coming to our rescue in times of need; no, not to help materially but certainly emotionally, psychically. This is what happened to a middle aged couple who had gone to New York to spend the Easter week end with their daughter in the University, and also to attend the Easter Mass at St Patrick's Cathedral to be celebrated by the Cardinal. It was a beautiful day. The three of them walked over to the Cathedral to attend the Mass in honor of their elder daughter who had been killed in an auto accident eight years ago. It was a very long que but still the three of them joined the line.

After waiting a while, the Mother asked the policeman if they would require tickets to attend the Mass. "Of course, you do need tickets. There is no way you can enter the Mass without them tickets."

The Family was deeply disappointed since it was too late to get the tickets. It was such a big crowd waiting in the que.

As they were about to leave the line a man came from nowhere and handed over an envelope to the Lady, saying: "Here, you take my tickets" and disappeared as suddenly as he had appeared. It was in such a quick flash that the family just did not see the man leaving, let alone thank him for the gesture. When the Lady opened the envelope she found four tickets — one white was for a seat in the center of the Cathedral, and the three yellow ones for the side gate. The crowd around the family was totally flabbergasted, as were the recipients of the noble gesture.

Their Daughter on the other side had sent a spirit-messenger to deliver the tickets and also informed her parents that she had a seat in the center of the Cathedral: the white ticket.

The old Mother's six children with their spouses came home for summer vacation. They were all sitting around the dinner table chatting away. Around midnight the Mother felt tired and went to bed, while the children continued talking of old memories. A couple of hours later the old Lady felt a finger-tap on her forehead. She knew it was her father who had passed on twenty one years earlier. She heard a voice internally urging her to go downstairs. So she did. She stood in the kitchen listening to her children talking. She could feel the presence of her father from the other side.

The kids were saying they certainly hoped that their children felt secure and nurtured and loved. Hearing this, the old Mother chirped in: "I sure hope you all know how much I loved each one of you when you were small!" — Silence, a sort of dead silence with a couple of faces even gone red! She thanked her Father from the other side for bringing her down and also for his presence. In the morning her Father showed up again and told her to let go the guilt. She was shown a slide show of the earlier days when her husband who was a recovering alcoholic came home dead-drunk one night after being sober for ten years. She was devastated. After that day it was downhill all the way. He lost his job, they got divorced and three children suffered cystic fibrosis, she had breast cancer. She worked two shifts to keep the family going and could hardly spend any time with the children. However the slide show went on and on. Her Father reminded her that the she was a good person and is still a good person, and that she had done the best that was humanly possible. So she must let the guilt go by.

In the morning the children came up to apologize. The Mother narrated her experience of the night before and told them it was the best thing to have happened. She felt at peace that her Father's intervention had brought ... Our deceased ones certainly know when we do need their help.

His nineteen year old son suddenly died in sleep from heart arrhythmia. The middle aged father could not believe that the young man was gone. He held on to him believing that somehow he could bring him back. One day when he was pulling weeds out of the grave his son's voice came out of the clear blue sky. It was a real happy loud and clear voice that told the father: "Dad, it is me. I wish you would turn me loose so that I could enjoy where I am. You and Mom always taught me and brought me up to be with God. Now you are keeping me from Him and from enjoying heaven ... I would appreciate if you would just turn me loose and let me enjoy it here."

The Father had always hated God. This encounter changed the man's whole life and restored his faith in God as ever before. Of Course, he let loose his departed son and his soul was at peace thereafter.

Their twenty seven year old son was murdered. The parents became leaders of "Parents of Murdered Children". Why do these innocent young children have to be murdered? God must answer this question: that was on the minds of all bereaved members of the Chapter.

One night she dreamed that she went to heaven and asked the Lord: Why did you allow my son to be murdered? The Lord said: "There is your Son. Go and let him welcome you." ... Her Son was there, standing in a corner, smiling with his arms held out to welcome her. He was in a dazzling white robe. There was happiness in his expression; he was radiant and his face just glowed. They just hugged and she wanted to squeeze him in her embrace. Just being there was sheer joy. In the process she just forgot her question "Why?" And then she woke up.

From this experience she learnt from the Lord that it is not important how we die and not to worry about the "Why?" What matters is how we live, and what the Lord gives his children.

A corporal in Force Recon at a Marine Base in Vietnam and his buddies were preparing to go out on a Mission. He went out for an evening walk and to pray. Suddenly, he noticed a haze about 20 odd feet in front of him, like a human coming closer to him and getting bigger. He took position on the ground ready to fire. But then he heard his father's voice: "You have made me proud. But where you are going on this mission you will need your full will power to return besides you will need your belief in yourself."

They were twelve of them. Around 3:30 A.M. the team headed out and was ambushed on the second day. Only three came back. The Corporal was one of them, seriously wounded in the chest while second guy had a minor wound in one arm and the third had a bullet in his leg. They carried the corporal almost eight miles to an LZ from where he was medically-evacuated. The Doctor had a quick look and remarked he doesn't have a chance to live and moved on to the other patients. The Corporal blacked out and had a funny feeling of being in between here and there. And he heard his father's voice: "It is not time to give up."

The corporal was shifted to another hospital in California a few weeks later, but still had many shell fragments in his chest. Nonetheless, he knew that it was not yet his time to pass away. The recent spiritual experience meant that his father had great love for him and that love carried on well after his death. He had therefore no doubt that he would pull through notwithstanding the initial remarks of the Doctor.

The Corporal was not the only one to have had such an experience; there were many more like him about whom he had heard. But they wouldn't go public with their stories lest they be dubbed as crazy! — There are numerous other stories narrated by the Guggenheims in their celebrated Book *Hello From Heaven* but I must call it a day here.

Peggy, wife of an officer in US State Department, was terribly upset over the sudden demise of her father. Since the husband could not accompany her for the last rites, she went alone to Fresno. On the return journey she fell asleep on the steering wheel. The car kept going at 40 MPH. When it neared a dangerous curve, her late father suddenly shouted at her to stop the car immediately. And that saved her life.

Two young girls Jane and Virginia were playing alone in their house in a posh locality of Washington. They got a call from the Hospital to come over immediately to identify a boy who was admitted in an emergency ward in a clinically unconscious state after an accident. A piece of paper in his pocket showed some telephone numbers one of which was of their father. The girls' mind raced back to their brothers. They were under great tension and rushed to the Hospital where they found that the person was one of the servants in their father's farmhouse. After making necessary arrangements they returned home and were surprised by another phone call, this time from their brother Fred who inquired if all was well at home since he had a gut-feeling that they were anxiously looking for him. — How could Jane's emotions be transmitted to Fred's heart? Paranormal alone can explain this coincidence.

Soon the other brother who was flying a helicopter over Richmond called home and enquired from Virginia if all was OK at home, since he had heard Jane's panicked voice hundreds of miles away at the same time. Such episodes reported from many different parts of the world bring to light enormous hidden capabilities of the human mind, as mentioned in Indian scriptures on yoga and spirituality.

The Ambassador of Turkey, Mr. Bullard Usakaligil used to live near our house. In 1938 he went on an official tour of Rumania. There he received the news of his brother's illness. He caught a train the same night to reach home and meet his ailing brother. The train was running in speed and he was fast asleep around midnight. Suddenly someone opened the door of his compartment and touched his hands. The strange visitor looked at his watch and said: Now, I am leaving you all, I just came to say last hello to you ..."

Mr. Bullard, now fully awake, switched on the light and saw the time as 5:00 AM. He reached home late in the evening with a heavy heart and learnt that his brother had passed away at exactly 5:00 AM that morning.[1]

Mr. Johnson was the US Ambassador to Japan during World War II. His wife had learnt Japanese. She and the children were sent away from Muckeden but the Ambassador stayed back since he had no orders to leave his post. On 7th December 1941 Japan bombarded Pearl

Harbor and arrested Mr. Johnson. On 7th March 1942 the neighbor in Laguna Beach California could receive direct broadcasts from the East. She informed Mrs. Johnson accordingly and told her to come over whenever she felt like listening to Japanese war bulletins. The Lady did not bother much about listening to Japanese news broadcasts. On 8th June Mrs. Johnson felt strangely restless. She felt as if her husband was calling her. At 9:50pm she knocked the neighbor's door and asked her permission to listen to Japanese news. Soon they were on to Muckeden radio station when some Japanese officers were speaking in English and announced that: Now you would listen to American Ambassador Mr. S. Johnson who announced the long awaited message that soon some POWs including himself would be exchanged from either side. "Whoever is listening to me kindly arrange to inform my wife that I am alright here and hope to be free soon." Some invisible power of the mind had already called her to listen to his message live at that very moment of time! What a fortunate coincidence, some would say; but the believers in spirituality would ascribe this to premonitions and psychic experience of an exceptional kind. People do get one to one communication in times of extreme emotional stress. The power of their minds charges their inner impulses leading to strange linkages giving rise to mental communication or precognitive experience "in the omnipresent medium of Consciousness."

References

1. Very interesting indeed!

19

Shambhala (*Imaginary Land of Heavenly Bliss*)

It is a Sanskrit word and Tibetans take it to mean "the source of happiness". While *Shambhala* is said to symbolise the hidden depths of the mind, the Kingdom of Tibet was, and the region of Tibet still is symbolic of spiritual enlightenment. Although the rest of the world believes that Shambhala is a mythical place of peace and spiritual bliss, a desired goal for an enlightened soul, Tibetans do believe that it is a real place in the planetary system, or hidden in a secret location deep within the Himalayas. However, some scholars believe without ascribing any credible evidence that Shambhala could possibly be a vestige of the ancient kingdom of Zhang-Zhung in Central Asia. Whatever it may be, the Lamas consider it as a 'Pure Land', a mystical kingdom that is the seat of most sacred and secret spiritual teachings of the world.

The *Kalachakra* (The Wheel of Time) that represents the highest and most esoteric of Tibetan Wisdom is also reposed in Shambhala origins of which are traced by the Buddhists to Siddhartha Gautama, the founder of Buddhism. Prior to his death he is said to have assumed the form of Kalachakra and delivered his secret teachings to a group in South India. Kalachakra is assumed to be a deity and Gautama is said to have taken the form of that deity. Eighty years old King Suchandra, purported to be the first king of Shambhala was one the audience who received the message from Gautama. According to the legend he wrote down the sermons verbatim and took them to Shambhala where he constructed the Kalachakra Mandala[1], the sermons and his commentaries.

Instructions for finding the hidden ancient Kingdom of Shambhala are said to be written in various Buddhist texts. The directions are rather obscure and only accomplished yogis are deemed capable of finding the place after great difficulties and exceptionally hard labor, and that too after flying over the snow capped peaks with the help of Siddhis (spiritual powers). However, the million dollar question still remains: Where is

Shambhala, if at all there is one. A Buddhist teacher writing in the 19th

Century mentioned North of Bodh-Gaya — a Buddhist shrine in the Bihar State of Northern India — as one of the probable sites.

It is claimed that the kingdom is hidden behind a ring of great snow mountains and is shaped like an eight-pedaled lotus blossom. Each of the eight regions is supposed to have twelve principalities. The capital of the Kingdom is Kalapa. It is located at its center and in turn is surrounded by a ring of snow-mountains. The Kingdom has gold covered pagodas and everything is hunky dory. All imagination runs wild!

Another source places the location in northern Tibet, in a land divided by eight mountain ranges. The capital is on top of Mount Kailash. Yet another source places the Kingdom in central Asia near River Oxus. In the context of Tibetan concept of six 'realms of beings' only two of which are perceptible to our physical senses, Shambhala, the legendary land of bliss of Eastern mythology is situated in the island of Britain, at Glastonbu[2] and not in the Gobi Desert as is generally believed.

Yet another concept of the Kingdom is that all its inhabitants became enlightened like the Buddha and it vanished from the earth while all its inhabitants went over to another celestial plane. Yet another version says that Rigden Pema Karpo, the last successor to King Suchandra will return to establish a universal Kingdom. The more the intellectual minds, the more the imaginary theories! In the words of Colin Wilson: "Men have a deeply ingrained habit of starting with the 'facts' they want to believe, and then working backwards to find the evidence to support them." It is not that all scientists go all out to support unpalatable fasts. Nevertheless, myth of the return to save humanity is common to many religions including the return of Jesus Christ and the final incarnation of Vishnu, Kalki, in Hinduism. According to Hindu philosophy the Universal Self is known as "Ishvara", and the personalised self as "Purusha", 'Man'. This function of the material world is called "Prakriti" encompassing five "Tatvas" which combine with three qualities of matter "gunas" — "Sattva", "Rajas" and "Tamas" — light, activity and darkness respectively.

The intensity and devotion of worship of Goddess Kali in Bengal are symbolic of relationship of *Shakti* to consciousness, the 'Purusha'. Shakti means female power, strength, energy of a deity personified as wife of a deity, the Purusha, the Man. Shakti is a feminine characteristic embodied in women[3], but not in men. The latter do have some Shakti as power of reproduction but the men lost the same in course of time.

References

1. A Buddhist or Hindu graphic symbol of the universe in the form of a circle enclosing a square within with a deity on each side.
   Edwin Bernbaum: *The Way to Shambhala*, New York, 1980
   Chogyam Trungpa: *Shambhala: The Sacred Path of the Warrior*; New York, 1984/86
2. Glastonbury is believed to be the nodal point of a number of lines of Ley that run straight connecting ancient sites, associated by some people with lines of earth energy
3. David Smith: *Hinduism and Modernity*; Blackwell Publishing; 2003; p. 109-110.

20

Totem: Personal Guardian Spirit

The modern religions and civilised societies have their God, gods and goddesses while tribal societies have their totem, a guardian spirit albeit, of late, many tribal societies have transformed their totem into the gods-goddesses of the type nearest to their advanced societies. For instance the northwest Indian, central and northeastern tribal societies have retained their totems but have also adopted the local gods-goddesses as their guardian spirits. It is part of the ongoing process of acculturation. for instance: the Kinners of Himachal Pradesh no longer believe in totems as their personal guardian spirits; instead they have their pantheon of gods and goddesses widely distributed all over Kinnaur district and its adjoining areas in Himachal Pradesh. The particular deity has well defined area of jurisdiction, ruling powers and a definite place in the semi-divine hierarchy with its status well established. Any negligence in worship of the deity, or obtaining its permission before embarking on a project, is considered the cause for any calamity like failure of crops, epidemics, lack of rain or excess thereof, etc. the supreme deity of Kinnauri pantheon is the goddess Devi

Chandrika. Her abode is in village Kothi of Kalpa subdivision and her jurisdiction extends well beyond that region. She is the supreme guardian spirit of every Kinnauri in her jurisdiction, like any totem in the northeastern tribal India. Guardian spirits are known by various names in different tribal societies. In Siberian Shamanism they are known as "tutelary spirits" while the Australian aborigines refer to their guardian spirit as the "spirit of the dead" and Mexican and Guatemalan Shamans call it Nagul.

A totem is essentially an animal form. It protects the tribe or clan on a collective basis as well as a person on an individual basis. A totem is essentially a sacred entity. A clan will not hunt its totem- animal. However, there is no bar in eating the meat of one's totem if it has been killed by some other clan. There is a deep rooted belief that the animal and human forms are related to one another in so far as the concept of totem is concerned. The totem in animal form can converse with humans. It is not necessary that the totem must always be in animal form which is generally the rule, but it might as well be in human form and that is where the usual gods-goddesses come into the picture. A totem is believed to possess magical-shamanistic powers by virtue of which it can perform extraordinary feats like making an animal, usually a wolf or tiger, to fly in the air to attack enemies of the tribe, or an individual for that matter. Some tribal cultures assume that males have guardian spirits right from their birth. Those who do not have their guardian spirit from birth generally do not grow to adulthood. Women do not generally have individual guardian spirits.

In order to become a shaman a person requires guardian spirits to get empowered so as to acquire the magical abilities to perform the role of a shaman. That is the inviolable rule of shamanistic societies. These spirits also serve as 'power animals' at the beck and call of the shaman. These spirits act as guardian angels for shamanistic journeys to underworld, as well for ascents upwards to the sky. Whatever it is, the guardian spirit is always protective of the shaman, never threatening or dangerous to the shaman. Nevertheless, guardian spirits do not remain attached to the same shaman; they change guard like on a sentry post. Acquisition of a guardian spirit is a process by itself. Some get it through dreams, hallucinogenic drugs, 'vision quest', via initiation rites for manhood, etc. Establishing contact with the guardian spirit is a series of rites by itself. Ecstatic dance is the usual format through which the person goes into a trance state and assumes the form of an animal.

Besides the guardian spirit, the shamanistic world also has a number of "spirit helpers". These are minor powers that perform such functions as curing illnesses. The Shaman uses these "helpers" collectively to achieve the desired results.

21

CHÖD
A Tibetan Rite of Impermanance

Medically Impossible, Totally Unbelievable, Most Unnatural but still TRUE!

You open any book on Tibet you are bound to come across some religious-spiritual experiences and episodes which are apparently out of the blues. The power of the mind is indeed phenomenal. The essential element in the process is total uninterrupted concentration on the subject occupying the mind. A person moving at incredible speed without application of any outside force the phenomenon of Tulpa, feats borne out of mind-control, cult of the dead, visions, matters of sate policy, fore warning and forecasts, and numerous such myriad issues – the list could well be interminably long.

The word chöd is of Tibetan origin, meaning 'to cut, to dismember'. It is derived from the Tibetan practice of disposing of the dead. There is hardly any wood to cremate a dead body as is the practice amongst the

Hindus of India. Nor it is a practical proposition in most parts of Tibet to dig a grave deep enough to bury the dead. Of necessity therefore the Tibetans had to resort to cut and dismember the dead body into small pieces and leave them at a place set apart for the purpose to be consumed by carrion-eating birds. Be that as it may, tantric rites are at the bottom of Tibetan, or Shamanistic, rite of self-dismemberment. The most interesting part of Chöd Rite is that it involves miraculous self-healing of the wound, literally within minutes, implying thereby the concept of "spiritual rebirth'. — So far so good. The other side of the coin is misuse and manipulation of the technique-philosophy of Chöd. Even many pre-communist Tibetans regarded this rite with suspicion in as much as it could lead to outright sorcery and necromancy of the Dug-pa cult which permitted its practitioners to indulge in divination to reanimation of the dead besides necrophilia, kidnapping of young girls for using them in rites involving sex-magic. Lest my comments here are misconstrued, I must clarify that such degeneration of the sacred Chöd Rite is restricted to a microscopic minority of Tibetan mystics and magicians.

The macabre ceremony of Tibetan Esoteric Tradition that I am going to describe now could well lay in the realm of some extremely extraordinary, virtually unbelievable, medically impossible, but all the same an absolutely true and verified story. It is indeed dangerous, so dangerous that it could lead to madness, or even real death.

The Tibetan 'Chöd Rite' is an enactment on a spiritual and psychological plane of self-mutilation and miraculous bodily healing of the practitioner of the rite. A Lama cuts himself open, take out his entrails, and place them before him after which he resumes his previous posture. Indeed very cruel and disgusting spectacle! But there it is, for all to watch and realise what power the

Lama possesses. The practice was quite common in the Lamaseries of Tartary in the nineteenth century. The Mongols refer to such a Lama s the 'Boktè'. He prepares himself for the formidable operation by fasting and praying over a prolonged period of time during which he must remain totally incommunicado with mankind and observe absolute silence. The initiate is generally equipped with a bell, Dorje, the ritual dart known as phurba, a small damaru-drum and a human thighbone trumpet called a kangling.

On the appointed day a multitude of pilgrims in the great court of the Lamasery where an altar is erected in front of the Temple gate. The moment of truth arrives when the Boktè, amidst the acclamations of the cheering crowd, seats himself on the altar, pulls out a large knife out of his girdle and places it on his knee. A large number of lamas are seated around him at his feet. They start reciting the terrible invocations of this frightful ceremony. As the recitation proceeds, the Boktè starts trembling in every limb, and gradually works himself up into phrenetic convulsions.

Concurrently, the waiting lamas too become quite excited. There is yelling, confusion and outcry. As this is going on, the Boktè suddenly throws aside the sacred scarf that envelops him, unfastens his girdle, and, seizing the sacred knife, slits open his stomach with one long cut. Streams of blood flow all over. The multitude prostrates before the frightful spectacle. Some question the Botkè about all sorts of hidden things, the future, destiny of the state and certain important personages, *et al*. The answers are noted and everyone takes them as the oracles.

When the showers of questions comes to an end, the lamas in attendance resume their incantations and prayers, but this time gravely, slowly, calmly and in rhythmic style. The Botkè collects the blood from the wound in his right hand, raises it to his mouth, breathes thrice upon it, and then throws it into the air with loud cries. Next, he rapidly passes his hand over the wound concurrently closing the wound with his bare hand. Soon everything is back to status quo ante, as pristine as it was with no trace of blood or the wound as if nothing had happened in the meantime. Of course, the only change in the situation is continuous prostrations by the multitude. The Boktè then rolls back his scarf around him and recites a short prayer of thanking the Almighty when all is over. The multitude starts dispersing. A few devout remain behind to contemplate and adore the blood-stained altar which the saint has quitted.

The foregoing account of the diabolical ceremony is not a fig of imagination, nor is it only one of its kind. There are many more such instances detailed accounts of which are available in many European writings on Tartary and Tibet. The ceremony I have described above was conducted in a Mongolian Lamasery in the presence of Father Abbè Huc and is told in his own words in his Book, Travels in Tartary, Thibet and China during 1844-1846. Since it was held in Mongolian, and not Tibet, and that too in the presence of a renowned Christian Father who had travelled extensively in Central Asia, it is all the reason to accept its authenticity, as opposed to the descriptions by other European writers. It would be of interest to note that, at that time, the Mongolian Lamasery was controlled by members of the 'Black Hat' Karmapa-sect which has recently made headlines in the Indian print media. This sect was strongly influenced by the Bon Faith as well as the Indian tradition of Tantra. On the other hand the Indian Saint Padmasambhava, the founder of Buddhism in Tibet remembered by Tibetans as Lopon Rinpoche. His faith later came to be known as the 'Red Hat' sect.

Since the same Botkè can perform the ceremony more than once, it stands to reason that the butchery may not involve the initiate's physical body; it might as well be a visionary trance nightmare. The doctrine of REINCARNATION is at the bottom of this cruel macabre rite. Nonetheless, it has a deep philosophical base too in as much as the physical body is as illusory as the ego-consciousness, the only reality being the mind.

The earlier biographical sketch (Thought-Forms and Exploits of Louis Eugene Alexandra Marie David) is a prelude to Alexandra undertaking the mystic diabolical Rite. During her stay in the desolate region she had the spiritual courage to undergo the most horrendous Chöd rite so as to truly imbibe the philosophy and concept of this extraordinary rite to which Tibetans accorded great importance in their myriad magical rites and ceremonies. Indeed, there was mysticism involved in the Rite in as much as the cutting and dismemberment of body parts was not only ritualistic but was also psychological without the body being actually involved in the process. All said and done, it is a matter of belief rather than a debate about the facts.

Among the first lessons taught by the Gomchen to his initiate was Milrepa's survival technique in the highlands' biting chill and cold. She quickly mastered the practice of body-heat-yoga, Tumo. In the process David–Neel was able to endure conditions as rigorous as any in the highlands of Tibet which she now entered in 1916 for the first time. This audacious action enraged the authorities in British India who expelled her from Sikkim on her return there, although her visit to Tibet was on a personal invitation from the Panchen Lama, a Monk second in authority to His Holiness the Dalai Lama. From Sikkim she managed to make her way to Japan, China and from there on to the Kumbum Monastery in Eastern Tibet.

22

Tumo

(Self Generation of Body Heat)

What is Tumo? This Tibetan word means simply as 'heat' or 'warmth', but only in the special sense of psychic heat. It is not an exclusively male prerogative (Madam David-Neel practiced this technique to survive in the extreme cold of Tibetan mountains). It is believed that an initiate requires three years, three months and three days of repeated strenuous exercises, both physical and mental, to acquire this art of self-generating of heat. However, it would be wrong to assume that strenuous exercises add to longevity; on the contrary, Tibetan lamas' efforts are generally geared towards shortening of life-span so as to achieve liberation from the cycle of birth, death and rebirth.

Tibetans recognise three types of Tumo[1]:

- The Tumo that arises spontaneously during ecstatic religious experience;
- Mystic Tumo which is the fire of bliss itself;
- Esoteric Tumo that keeps the adept physically warm.

Thopaga was a Tibetan born in 1052 near the border with Nepal. He lost his rich father, a merchant, at age seven and his uncle grabbed all the family property. When Thopaga grew up, he came in contact with an evil teacher who taught him black magic. Thopaga decided to take revenge on his uncle. At the wedding of his uncle's son Thopaga used black magic to destroy the house where all the guests for the wedding had assembled. Thirty five persons died in Thopaga's black-magic episode from which Thopaga spared his uncle and aunt so that they might endure further suffering. Urged on by his mother Thopaga conjured a hail storm to destroy his Uncle's crops thus effectively ruining him. When he was approaching middle age he decided to reform himself and apprenticed himself to a saintly teacher named Marpa, the founder of the Kargyut-pa School of Tibetan Buddhism, who refused to initiate him until he had atoned for his past sins through a regular regime of severe physical punishment for almost six years. The rigorous regime of regular beatings and back-breaking tasks also involved repeatedly building and tearing down a stone house[2]. Marpa initiated the disciple only after the latter reached age forty-four. Thopaga saw the death of his mother in a dream after which he decided to devote his life towards attainment of life's ultimate spiritual goal — liberation from the cycle of birth, death and rebirth generated by karmic action. Hindus call this liberated state as nirvana while the Tibetans refer it as "entering the clear light". However, Thopaga decided that after he attains nirvana he would renounce that state until all sentient beings had achieved enlightenment. In other words he was determined to become a Buddha.

It is wrong to believe that there was only one Buddha, Prince Gautama. Buddha means "Enlightened One" and certainly there could be more than one, a chain of enlightened ones over a period of time.

With his new resolve in mind Thopaga took up residence in the totally seclude White Cave in the Horse's Tooth in the high altitude mountains. This is where Tumo comes in — a severe mental discipline that generates great body heat for the human body to survive the rigors of extreme cold. He wore only a light cotton robe known as repa in Tibetan which gave him the name Milarepa. His sole source of sustenance was soup made from nettles which eventually gave his skin and hair a greenish tinge. In the process he developed curious powers through which he could leave his body at will and travel anywhere not only in this world but in other realms too, besides the ability to metamorphose into different forms of animals also.

When Milarepa died he resurrected himself in a second body which sang hymns amidst the flames of his humeral pyre. After the flames of the pyre died there was no sign of Milrepa's bones or ashes.

That is exactly what had happened in the case of Guru Nanak, Saint-Founder of the Sikh Faith, born on April 15, 1469 in a Hindu Family at village Talwandi Rai Bhoe subsequently renamed Nankana Saheb, now in Pakistan about 65 km North-West of Lahore. His elder sister, Bibi Nanki perceived in him the light of God. Indeed, Nanak was the embodiment of Divine light but Bibi Nanki did not reveal the secret to anyone. After Nanak received the vision he went wandering about the countryside in search of Truth and Reality. His constant Muslim companions, Mardana and Bala kept him company.

In order to curb the frequent communal riots between Hindus and Muslims, and large scale killings and forcible conversion of the Hindus by the Muslims, in the later part of the fifteenth century Guru Nanak initiated a truly genuine secular movement. However, his valiant efforts at reconciliation of the two antagonistic communities proved a pipe dream although both treated Nanak as their Saint.

Guru Nanak died on September 22, 1539 at an auspicious time of early hours of the morning. In the manner of spiritual masters of Tibeto-Buddhism, Nanak knew that his time had come. His Muslim followers wanted to bury him while the Hindus wanted a proper cremation since Nanak was born a Hindu and died as a Hindu. Both worshipped him and both claimed the right to the dead body for final death rites Soon it developed into a serious contentious issue between the two communities. Lest the matter gets out of control the Guru is reported to have told the congregation: "You place flowers on either side of my body, the Hindus on the right and Muslims on my left. Those whose flowers remain fresh tomorrow morning will have their way." The congregation was then asked to pray after which the Guru pulled a white sheet over his body. Next morning when the sheet was raised the congregation was totally flabbergasted; there was no sign of the Body or any parts thereof! And the flowers of both communities were fresh as ever which they reverently collected.[3]

No doubt, Baba Nanak was Guru for the Hindus (later Sikhs), Pêr se for the Musalmans and Lama for the Tibetans.

References

1. Brennan, J.H.: Occult Tibet: Secret Practices of Himalayan Magic; Llewellyn Publications, USA, 2002; p. 59.
2. This structure, in Southern Tibet was still standing in the 20th Century as vouched by J.H. Brennan, op. cit. p. 15.
3. Gulati N. Mahinder: *World's Youngest Religion SIKHISM: Islamic Influence and Tibetan Connection*; Atlantic Publishers, 2007, New Delhi.

23

Spirit World

Séance literally means a "sitting". It is a gathering of spiritually inclined like-minded persons for a metaphysical experience — to hear what the spirits have to say on certain matters through the voice of the "medium". In other words the object is to make contact with spirits of the deceased in order to obtain information from them. The medium is merely an instrument of the spirits and not the originator of the communications, or form thereof — clairvoyance or direct voice, whether such physical phenomena as Apport might be apparent — the entity that exercises control over the proceedings as to what spirits are coming into the medium, or going out for that matter, like an MC at a social function, so to say — that entity is generally called the 'Controller", for which the gentler dignified term is the "Spirit Guide". In spiritualist literature apport is an object that has been brought into the séance room as if out of thin air by the spirit guide, falling from the air above. Initially it might even be hot to touch since after it has been dematerialised, teleported through space, and then rematerialised in the séance room. The apport can be anything – a small precious stone, a piece of jewelry, a book, a vase, a flower or even a small bird.

Initially it might even be hot to touch since after it has been dematerialised, teleported through space, and then rematerialised in the séance room. Some apport may suddenly appear on a table in the middle of the sitters! In spiritualist literature apport are things that appear as if from nowhere, objects that fall from the air. These are frequently associated with poltergeist activity.

Another term used in this context is the GATEKEEPER, a personal spirit-guide of the medium. This guide oversees the coming and goings of the spirits who want to make contact with the medium at a séance. He or she makes sure that the spirits are there at the right time and helps them in making contact with the medium. Of course the usual function of the 'gatekeeper' to keep out the unwanted spirits falls in his/her jurisdiction. More often than not, these Gatekeepers and spirit-guides are in the form of Native Americans.[1]

GUIDES and GUARDIAN-ANGELS

Whenever there is some confusion about the proceedings, or some answer given by the medium, the control steps in and clarifies the position. But a control is not an all knowing entity. Sometimes he may not be able to sort out the confusion which he readily admits and asks someone else for clarification. Incidentally, all controls or spirit-guides are not males even though most are; female spirit-guides are also known to have controlled séances.

It is not that all séances-apports have a happy ending. William Stanton Moses has recorded some serious blunders by controls. In one instance perfume was supposed to be produce for the sitters to enjoy. Instead a stinking odor came out. It was so bad that the sitters had to vacate the room and the event called off. In yet another similar incident, dense smoke filled the room with the same results. Usually, whenever any such untoward incident occurred, the controller would call off the séance and the medium would come out of trance.[2]

Guardian Angels are also called 'guardian spirits', tutelary spirits, protective spirit, etc. There are also guardian spirits known as 'genius loci' which is supposed to protect a particular place. Some communities believe that every person is born with his/her own specific guardian angel right from the moment of birth while others believe they appear only when there is a specific need for them. Obviously, the chief function of a guardian angel is to protect him and ensure that he/she follows a positive and productive life. In other words, in spiritualism guardian angel is synonymous with chief spirit guide, or the Gatekeeper. In the Old Testament it is mentioned that 10-12 angels keep a watch over different kingdoms at people, while the Muslims believe that every person is guarded by two angels by day and another two by night.[3]

Principle 2 in the Declaration of Principles of National Spiritualist Association of Churches states: "We believe that the phenomena of nature, both physical and spiritual, are the expression of Infinite Intelligence." The NSAC Spiritual Manual interprets this to mean:" In this manner we express our belief in the immanence of spirit and that all forms of life are manifestations of Spirit of Infinite Intelligence, and thus that all men are children of God." This is what we have as the closest definition of Spirit that we have from the Western spiritual literature – albeit not a very satisfactory definition. It is therefore necessary to analyse the characteristics of the "spirit", its attributes and dwelling.

The body is constituted of three principles: physical body, soul and spirit the "triune being" animated by the 'Universal Spirit', the 'Infinite Intelligence'. In this context:

- Spirit is the highest and the innermost principle;

- Soul is the spiritual body and the intermediate principle;
- Physical body is the material or outermost principle acting as the clothing and vehicle for first two.

By implication, spirit is indestructible since it is the "inmost principle, the divine particle, the vital essence, the inherent actuating element in life" as has been described in the *Encyclopedia of Psychic Science, 1933*. The spirit dwells in the astral body or the soul. In fact, in many religious philosophies spirit and the soul mean one and the same thing. The terms are interchangeable. According to Thomas Grimshaw: "Spirits are real people., human beings – men, women and children stripped of their outer garment of flesh, but still possessed of a real, substantial body that was known as the 'spiritual body."[4] Indian Philosophy said the same thing more than a couple of millenniums back when Shri Krishna in his second discourse to Arjuna, said:

"He is not borne, nor doth he die;

nor having been, ceaseth he any more to be;

Unborn, perpetual, eternal and ancient,

He is not slain when the body is slaughtered. (20)

As a man, casting off worn-out garments, taketh new ones,

So the dweller in the body, casting off worn out bodies, Entereth into others that are new." (21)

Spirits can manifest in various forms through materialisations making use of a medium's ectoplasm, Apports, Psychokinesis etc. Native Americans make hardly any distinction between spirits and ghosts. Perhaps, they are right.

Believe it or not, *Spirit World* is a real world. It is as real to the spirits functioning in their spirit bodies as the physical world is to us in this mortal world. In fact, spirit world is the new place where we make our homes after we transit from the Earth Plane to the 'Other Side'. That new world has no demarcated boundaries in terms of space, time and tangibility, nor any divisions in terms of heaven or hell. It is just one place neither good nor bad. Over there, there are no rewards or punishments either.

Many details of the Spirit World have been found in the various accounts of NDE. 'Medium' Mary T. Langley delivered a trance-address at Los Angeles, California. The same was reproduced in the Spiritual Manual issued by NSAC.

SPIRIT LIGHTS

These are frequently seen as dancing globules or sparks of light indicating thereby that spirit is present in the room. It is on record that when Dr. Gustav Geley conducted a séance with the Polish medium Franek Kluski on May 15, 1921, he reported a luminous trail, about half a meter long, oscillating about a meter above and behind his head. It lasted about a minute, disappeared and reappeared again and again several times. In the same vein, Shamanistic tradition has little dots of light called 'sparkies' – often blue, purple, or silver — that appear before a healer after he has done his work.

In the field of SPIRITUAL HEALING, more often than not, it is a deceased physician or surgeon who comes through the medium to suggest the line of treatment. Often, the spirit guide of the medium actually works through the patient, particularly if it happens to be a surgical problem.

SPIRIT PHOTOGRAPH

These have been in vogue for more than a century and a half. These are also called psychic photographs – pictures of the deceased one in their after-life. The story goes that one day in 1861 William H. Mumler of Boston, Massachusetts was tinkering with his equipment. With nothing better to do he tried to take a picture of himself. But to his utter surprise the picture that came out showed Mumler with a young girl sitting beside him on a chair. He wrote on the back of that picture

"This photograph was taken of myself, by myself, on Sunday, when there was not a living soul in the room besides me, so to speak. The form on my right I recognise as my cousin, who passed away about twelve years since."

Spirit photographs are subject to easy fraud. These are therefore no longer in favour. Instead, Infrared stills and video images are now in vogue. Ghost Research Society of Oak Lawn, Illinois, collects spirit photographs from around the world. These pictures are scrutinised, analysed, scanned and then fed into a computer system for digitizing. In this manner even the minutest details can be examined. Some of these pictures are synonymous with "thought-photography".

SPIRITUAL COMMUNICATION got a big boost from latest technology in communication systems. The American Association of Electronic Voice Phenomena (AA-EVP) was founded by Sarah Estep in 1982 "to provide objective evidence that we survive death in an individual conscious state." The members of AA-EVP maintain that the spirits of the dead can, and do have, such evidence through the various devices now in vogue—telephones, tape recorders, answering machines, computers, radios, cameras, et al.

References

1. Barbanell Maurice: This is Spiritualism; the Spiritual Press, USA, 1959.
2. Raymond Buckland: The Spirit Book; op, cit. p. 80; based on Fodor Nandor: *Encyclopedia of Psychic Science,* London, Arthur Press, 1933.

3. Cavendish Richard (ed.): *Man, Myth and Magic: An Encyclopedia of the Supernatural*, London, BPC, 1970.
4. Grimshaw Thomas: *General Course of the History, Science, Philosophy and Religion of Spiritualism* (1973).

24

Evil Forces

Since times immemorial mankind has believed in the existence of forces of evil, right or wrong. This has been all the more pertinent amongst the tribal communities all over the world, and continues to be so believed even in modern times, notwithstanding the process of acculturation through contacts with the advanced societies. Demons, ghosts, spirits, are all part and parcel of the occult belief system. How to use the endless list of these evil forces, or how to tame them, all form part of the folklore? These practices are still prevalent in many parts of the world, even amongst some half-educated societies. "*Toona*", in the vernacular of many parts of India, is practiced in various odd manners and via numerous techniques. In fact, the word devil has its root in the Hindu word "Deva", an angel or a shining one. However, there is no specific evidence to prove the existence of evil forces, albeit proof of existence of ghosts and evil spirits does have backing of a number of scientific investigations.

Here I might as well cite two recorded cases of evil forces in action —After a late night party turned into an impromptu séance, a man named Bill Slater (later to become head of BBC Television drama) left and went off to flirt with a pretty girl. After he went off to bed in his flat in the early hours of the morning, he found himself half awake feeling as if some kind of presence was amassing itself on his chest, making every effort to take over his mind and body. This spiritual tussle went on for nearly twenty minutes before Slater could get rid of the presence. He was utterly exhausted after the struggle. It was indeed a startling tale of possession, possibly caused by someone who got infuriated at Slater's flippancy at the party and directed a beam of ill-will at him. This sort of activity is reported in another instance from St Leonard on Sea:-

"So years ago my husband was treated very badly by the man he worked for. We had been to his house, and I knew the room where he slept. This night I was feeling a lot of anger and hate, and felt myself concentrating very hard on the side of the bed which I thought he would be sleeping on; I was sticking pins into his stomach slowly, one by one. I heard the next morning that his wife had been taken to hospital early hours of that morning in terrible pain. They thought it was gall-stones, but the tests showed nothing wrong. Did I do that, do you think? I know I felt drained the next morning because I had concentrated so much ..."[1]

Many societies still believe that concentrated ill-will against a certain person, for whatever reason, can have a maleficent effect. In an astral body one could travel light-years into the void of space fueled only by the power of thought.[51] According to Acharya Shriram Sharma, clusters of thoughts have their distinct colors! Thoughts of hatred, lust, jealousy, revenge, et al, have a dark black hue while fear and anxiety exhibit brownish aura. Pure love is reflected in bright red, and so on. The power of thought or the power of Mind is indeed mind boggling! Nonetheless, in the astral body memory falters the OBE traveler.

Human mind is such a vast realm than man ever thought possible. You can explore its latent powers only if you start believing strongly that such powers do exist, and are merely waiting to be explored and tapped. It is the positive attitude of optimism that would open the gates to power of the mind supernatural.

The most interesting and convincing proof of the mystery of life is the existence of poltergeist. Poltergeists are of human origin. This discovery is a great landmark in the history of human intellectual development. Each one of us has multi-levels of intellect varying anywhere between low,-medium to high.

DEMONS and DEVILS

In the course of this narrative these topics have been touched upon, in one form or the other. It is now time to take a comprehensive view of these elements of the spirit world. Before we do that, let's clearly define what we mean by these three different phrases, which on the face of it, appear to mean one and the same thing.

Mankind has believed in demonology for millennia. It made no difference whether their cultural origins were primitive or advanced, educated or otherwise. Irrespective of the level of intellectual development belief in, and practice of, demonology continued unabated. Essentially, all three are evolutionary products of 'Satan', based on elaborate cosmology of heaven and hell, totally evil in character. Demons are immortal. Their origin lies in angels, whose souls have gone terribly astray, deviated from the normal path of transit from the mortal world to the "Other Side". They perform endless variety of functions and it is virtually impossible to classify them according to their respective functions. Their usual technique of exercising power over humans is to lure them into wickedness by actually entering human bodies and consequently their minds to do their wicked biddings. They are powerful beings giving rise to sorcery, superstition, exorcism of possession by spiritual means, et al. Christian demonology has classified them according to their habitat — 'fiery': those who dwell in the upper air; 'aerial': who inhabit the air around us; 'terrestrial': those cast away from heaven to permanent exile to planet earth; 'aqueous': those living in water; 'subterranean: who dwelt in caves and caverns; and lastly are the 'heliophobic' demons who hate light and never appear in daytime. Accordingly certain demons were given names – *Utukku*: the spirit of the dead who haunted places; *Alu*: the spirit of disaster, half human half animal, who dwelt in desolate ruins; *Ekimmu*: the spirit of suicide and violent death who roamed the earth looking for possible victims; *Gallu*: the spirit of nightly assaults and attacks; and so on and so forth ending with *Shabriri* who brought about blindness.[3]

According to Sylvia Leek[4]: "A demon can be broadly defined as an anonymous god, a personification of one or another of certain vague and less definable powers that exerted influence with the major deities." That may be so. However, the Zoroastrian (Persian) religion is concerned more with the eternal conflict between good and evil, between the good god Mazda, and the bad god Ahriman — a duality of godheads as opposed to Christian belief in monotheism. Eastern religions, particularly Indian, were, and still are, largely polytheistic in which the ancient Vedic ritual of sacrifice and sharing the sacrificial meal with many devas (supernatural beings) to propitiate them for personal material benefits. No wonder therefore that the Vedic universe is populated with benevolent and malevolent supernatural beings, the latter category may be assumed as personification of demons and evil spirits. In fact, some people believe that demons are not mere spirits;

they do have bodies of sorts, of ethereal nature, usually invisible unless they decide to make themselves visible. If we accept this hypothesis it would mean they had human needs like food and drink. Their favourite food is believed to be sacrificial smoke from human and animal sacrifices which were practiced on a large scale in the middle ages, and much later too. I might as well mention that there are innumerable descriptions of demons and devils as personally perceived by saints and laity alike — looking like attractive females to pervert the saints, or as young handsome men to corrupt the females, and so on. Going a step further, demons could also take the form of animals or even as inanimate objects.

In the words of Anthony Finlay: "One puzzling question (among many!) is why the powerful spirits like the demons and their master the Devil should think it appropriate to enter into man – day or night." Your answer would be as good or bad as mine! However, according to Origen demons attack men in two ways: by possession, and second by attacking humans with evil thoughts. To me both appear to be two sides of the same coin. Be that as it may, devil worship is a historical fact arising out of fear of the unknown when Man lacked knowledge of most phenomena on planet earth.

The Devil is essentially the innovation of Christianity and Islam, originally an angel gone astray, later turned into a somewhat bad spirit, mostly malevolent but sometimes benevolent too. There may be thousands of them inhabiting various nooks and corners, haunting so to say, the places of their habitation. They are afraid to transit through the proverbial 'tunnel of light' for fear of severe punishment for their evil deeds and therefore prefer to remain earth-bound.

In most cultures death is highly inauspicious leaving behind a lingering fear of pollution for the bereaved family besides the danger of the household being haunted by a malevolent ghost, particularly so if the dead person was not well treated by the household during its lifetime. The age old Aryan practice of sacrificial fire is adopted to ward off the evil consequences of death. Hindus have adopted cremation as the sacrificial fire to cleanse the polluted environment, thereby allowing the spirit of the dead to smoothly transit on its way out. I shall refrain from the elaborate funeral rites which may differ from region to region, community to community. However, the basics are: The corpse is bathed, anointed, wrapped in a white cloth and placed on funeral pyre with feet pointing south towards the realm of Yama (the god of death) and head pointing north, the realm of Kubera (the god of wealth). The fire is lit and the corpse is reduced to ashes, to be collected ceremoniously later and disposed off according to the practice of the sect or community. Rice balls are offered to the departed soul for ten days recapitulating the ten lunar months of the embryo's gestation.

WITCHCRAFT

This narrative would remain incomplete without at least a cursory reference to witchcraft. Christian tradition ascribes the institution of witches-witchcraft to the first century A.D. and that it flourished in most parts of Europe during the fourteenth and seventeenth centuries taking on an extremely savage level of persecution, torture to extract a confession that was considered enough to declare the woman guilty, and then to eliminate her by some hideous means. The witch had to be eliminated completely since she was an embodiment of the Devil, exercising her power through the demons to bring about extraordinary misfortune to the community. However, if we go back to what I may call as the 'anthropological times' we notice that witchcraft is as old as the Man on this planet. It was prevalent even in stone-age. The basis of this tradition was pure and simple superstition arising out of fear of the unknown since early man could not fathom the vagaries of nature and the celestial phenomena.

This unfortunate trend continued unabated till well after the pre-literate tribal societies turned a corner for closer association with the so called advanced societies. The essential basis for witchcraft is the presence of a woman, the accused, and the accuser (a male) who may be harboring some personal grudge against the woman. Some sort of social relationship, of whatever nature, between the accused and the accuser is sine qua non for witchcraft to flourish. Anthropologist Evans-Pritchard mentions that "in a study of Azande witchcraft we must bear in mind, firstly, that the notion (of witchcraft) is a function of misfortune, and secondly, that it is a function of personal relations."[5] In the same vein, Scarlett Epstein while researching in a Mysore village concluded that as women have entered the field for economic struggle independently of their men folk, has given rise to social tensions and cross accusations of witchcraft.

The Mundas believe that the '*dianes*' or witches have to undergo training to acquire the secret knowledge of the secret art. This learning process is carried out at dead of night when witches from different villages gather at a fixed spot to pool their knowledge. They perform awe-inspiring rites, dance and sing till early morning, become naked and bathe in a nearby pool of water. "The nakedness of a woman is forbidden and is considered symbolic of evils of a Daine. The Mundas strongly believe that if one meets her at that time, the person may fall seriously ill, or even may die. People cannot say how witchcraft works ... but know better what to do when such a case occurs!" Buddhadeb Chaudhuri The author has personally investigated two specific cases from

Midnapur district of Bengal and found that in both of these casehistories, personal misfortunes personal and grudges had given rise to witchcraft accusations. It is also called necromancy in more sophisticated terminology, which also means black magic or the ability to talk to the dead.

Witches do not exist per se; they do so only in the mind of the person who has suffered a personal misfortune. Generally, old widowed women living alone with no male are accused of being witches. When someone is seriously ill, or his loved near and dear one is wasting away, he tries to find out who could possibly have ill will towards him – the result: an accusatory finger towards a witch!

References

1. Collin Wilson: op. cit. p. 452.
2. Albert Taylor: op. cit. pp. 47-48.
3. Anthony Finlay: Demons! Blandford, Strand, London
4. Sylvia Leek: *Drawing Out the Devil,* W.H. Allen, London, 1976.
5. Evans-Pritchard, E.E.; *Witchcraft, Oracles, and Magic among the Azande*, Clarden Press, Oxford, 1937; p. 106.

25

Death - Transition or Terminus?

Death has been accepted as end of a living being. This is considered as a fundamental fact of life ever since the dawn of civilisation. But have we ever given thought to the questions: What is death? What element(s) of a human being die when the so called death occurs? What happens to them when the physical body is disposed off? Where do we go when we die, if at all we go anywhere? Is death the ultimate end of a human being? A Terminus like the end of railway line Delhi-Haridwar-Dehradun, or a branch line Delhi-Haridwar-Rishikesh going deep into *Dev Bhoomi* with numerous pilgrimage centers dotted all over? Or is death a mere transition to another form of life, like the branch line? Till lately, Western civilisation had no answers to these pertinent but natural questions, while they knew very well that death was, and still is inevitable. On the other hand, the Eastern philosophy had known the answers and a lot more, over a period of millennia.

Death is certainly not a terminus; it is merely a transition from one form of life to another, generally human but could well be in an altogether different domain too. Yes, that is what death really is—a transition to the “Other Side” in preparation for a rebirth. It is inevitable. And if we know that death is a certainty, and so is Rebirth, then why are we afraid of the inevitable end! Lord Krishna in Úrimad Bhagavad Gitâ in His battlefield-sermon to Arjuna said:-

For the soul there is neither birth nor death;

Nor does it come into existence after having been born.

It is unborn, eternal, constant and primeval.

It is not killed even when the body is slain. Discourse II, Verse 20)

As a person discarding worn-out clothes puts on new ones,

So an embodied soul casting off old bodies

Enters into others which are new. Verse 22)

Since death is not the ultimate end for the soul, it simply means that only the gross body dies. It is only the biological existence of the body that comes to an end with the death of the person. Now in so far as the anatomy and biology is concerned all humans are alike. But that is where the similarity ends. Bodily characteristics, psychological make-up and intellectual talents are widely varying factors in different human beings, racial stocks, regional characteristics, etc. These factors lay the founding of the personality of a person, besides being vital considerations in dealing with health of the gross body. Our spiritual, or astral body is still far more complicated besides being far more subtle; IT is on a much higher plane above the gross body.

Weapons cannot cut the soul, nor can fire burn it,
Water cannot drench it, nor can wind make it dry.
(Verse 23)

For certain is death for the born,
And certain are birth for the dead;

Therefore do not grieve over the inevitable.

INTERMEDIATE STATE:
BARDO ANTARABHAVA (Verse 27)

According to Buddhist view, "life consists of a series of successive states of consciousness: the first is the Birth-Consciousness and the last is the Death-Consciousness. The interval between the two states of Consciousness is the period during which transformation from the 'old' to a 'new' being is effected; Tibetan philosophy calls this "*Bardo*", or the intermediate state, while in Hindu philosophy it is *Antarábhâva*. The dying consciousness is continued into a short term body called *Gandharva*, which lasts for seven days, or seven times seven days, the forty-nine days of the Bardo. There is great esoteric significance behind the forty-nine days of the Bardo, the square of the sacred number Seven. The number seven has long been a sacred number amongst the Aryans and many other races. Its use in the Revelation of John illustrates this, as does the conception on the seventh day being regarded as holy. According to occult teachings of Northern Buddhism and Higher Hinduism there are seven worlds or seven degrees of Maya which constitute the seven globes of a planetary chain. On each globe there are seven rounds of evolution taking the total to forty-nine stations of active existence. It is believed that presently we are in the Fourth Round in which there are four kingdoms of living creatures: Those are:

Element Fire

Element Air

Element Water

Element Earth

The Earth-Element of the Third Day produces the solid constituents of the human form while the Fire Element of the Fourth Day produces the animal-heat of Attachment i.e., Lust. Finally, the Element Air of the

Fifth Day produces the breath of life. After the fifth day the Bardo visions become less and less divine. At that stage the after-death dream ends exhausting the Intermediate State when he passes into equally illusory rebirth in human form, or any of the many mansions of existence.

The transition to next birth, the nature and quality of rebirth, is governed by a person's accumulated karmic debt, the outstanding debt of all previous lives that is carried forward to the new life, all added together, to be repaid in the new birth, however long or short that may be.

DEATH CEREMONIES[56]

Death is not an event, nor is it a terminus; in fact it is a process of transition to the "Other Side". It is only the body that has died, but the being continues to be alive. Several minutes after the heart stops beating the doctors can still record a mini-ECG by probing for signals inside the cardiac cavity. Life does not cease all at once in one go; cellular death is long delayed. We live in a transient world whose essence is impermanence. When a Hindu dies, his "essential being" (the soul) remains Hindu and his ghost craves for Hindu funeral rites. So it goes with other Faiths. The souls do not lose their belief system on account of death of the body. This is the Indian view, right or wrong. — A story goes that when a European-planter in Malabar died, he was buried by his friends but his ghost kept causing trouble to the people around. A witch doctor was consulted who advised that the ghost craved for his favourite whisky and beer since he was habituated to these drinks during his life-time. In order to propitiate the troubled spirit, the people started pouring over the grave the same brands of whisky and beer which the sahib was used to. This restored tranquility in the area!

According to Birthed Vishnu Purana Hindus speak of 8,400,000 graded kinds of births in low forms of beings before culminating in Man. If the opportunity now provided is misused through misconduct or neglect, it is well on the cards that that soul shall transmigrate into lower forms of being, the best of which might as well be in animal kingdom. However, some people withdraw from the "clear light" state and remain earth bound in order to fulfill their desires in the life just extinguished. They are the ghost-bodies and the place becomes haunted.

When the death symptoms are complete a white cloth is thrown on the face. No one is permitted to touch the corpse so that the process of separation of the Bardo body from its earth-counterpart is complete. This process is believed to take approximately one-half to four days. All doors and windows of death-chamber are closed and absolute silence is maintained. The priest examines the 'Aperture of Brahma' on the skull to see if the spirit has departed, which it should normally have done by this time. Meanwhile the astrologer-lama casts the death-horoscope based on the moment of death. He determines the proper method of disposal of the corpse, time and manner of the funeral and the rites to be performed. Then the corpse is tied in a sitting posture and placed in a corner of the death chamber. Meanwhile, relatives and friends of the deceased have started assembling. They are fed and entertained to no end. After the funeral the lamas who read the Bardo Thodol return to pray before the effigy of the deceased kept in the corner of the death chamber once a week until the forty-nine days of the Intermediate State have ended. During this period fresh food is place daily before the effigy (as it used to be in ancient Egypt — 'statue of Osiris' — to which the similarity is most striking). Depending on the circumstances of the family, the rites may cease on the fourteenth day, or the twenty-first day, or even right up to forty-nine days.

SIX STATES OF BARDO

- The natural state of Bardo while in the womb;
- The Bardo of the Dream-state;
- The Bardo of the ecstatic equilibrium while in deep meditation;
- Bardo of the moment of death;
- Bardo during experiencing of the Reality;
- Bardo of inverse process of sangsaric existence.

The rites concerning the effigy are a relic of the Bön religion prevalent in Tibet before the advent of Buddhism. At the termination of funeral rites the face – paper of the effigy is ceremoniously burnt in the flame of a butter lamp, and the spirit of the deceased is given a final farewell. By the color of the flame and the way in which the flame acts the after-death fate which the deceased has met is determined." When one year has elapsed after the death, a feast is given in honor of the deceased after the widow is free to remarry.[57] Connected with the funeral there is an interesting ritual. The officiating lama presents a 'scarf of honor' to the corpse while removing it from the house. He addresses the corpse, advises it freely partake of the offered food and warns it that it is dead and that its ghost must not haunt the place or trouble living relatives, and to take the right path— the white one. "Come this way!" While leading the funeral procession he holds one end of the long scarf while the other is tied to the corpse. The chief lama who leads the procession rings a hand-bell while another intermittently blows the sacred conch shell. From time to time the chief lama looks back to invite the spirit to accompany the body and to assure it the route is in the right direction.

In Tibet various methods of disposing of the corpse are in vogue. Cremation is followed only by the rich who can afford the fuel; otherwise the corpse is chopped to pieces on a desolate hilltop and left for the birds and beast of prey. After a length of time when all flesh is gone the bones are hammered into bits in small rock-cavities, mixed with flour and then given to birds to devour. The Tibetan air-burial is thus more thorough than that of the Parsees of Bombay in India.

THE JUDGMENT[58]

The Tibetan and Egyptian Judgment Scenes have so much in common as to suggest common origins for which history as yet has no explanation — The Tibetan version has Dharma Raja (Shinje-chho-gyal) King of the Dead, commonly called Yama-Raja holding Court weighs the black pebbles placed on one side and the white ones on the other symbolically weighing the evil and the good deeds with the heart representing the conduct or conscience of the deceased. Present before the monkey headed Shinje are various deities, some animal headed and some human headed, and they constitute the jury. The judgment in every case is meted out by the impartial *Shinje* while the *Yama*, the Hindu god of the dead, consults the mirror of Karma in which the naked soul is reflected. Shinje weighs out the good as opposed to the evil deeds (white and black pebbles).

In Buddhist view there are five messengers of death. Each one conveys an advance warning of inevitability of death, the law of karma taking its own course and cautions the subject to refrain from evil deeds. Few heed the warning signals and suffer as a consequence.

THE COSMOGRAHY

The sacred Mount Meru (Ri-rab in Tibetan) is the central core around which Hindu and Buddhist cosmography is structured. Mt. Meru is believed to extend for eighty thousand miles above the Central Enchanted Ocean. The Mount extends the same distance below the surface of the Ocean which itself is reported to be 80,000 miles deep and the same distance wide. Mind boggling dimensions indeed! But so is the Cosmos. The cosmos is considered to be disposed in seven concentric circles of oceans, each circle being separated by an equal number of intervening concentric circles of 'golden' mountains. They are believed to be the central hub that supports the entire vast infinite cosmos of all the worlds — a gravitational center of the known universe, and beyond. How far beyond cannot be fathomed by human mind. The continents are believed to lie outside the seven circles of oceans and mountains. No one has seen these circular structures, nor any one is likely to; nonetheless the concept persists to explain the cosmography of the universe. Below lay the hells and above are the heavens supported by Mount Meru. All the hells and heavens are graded according to divine will. Of course the best on top is the Nirvana.

Within Mt. Meru itself there are four realms, one above another. The three lower ones are inhabited by various genii while the fourth is reserved for the fallen ungodly spirits, the Asuras, who are constantly waging wars against the gods above.

The concept of infinite fathomless universe implies that beyond one such universe lies another, yet another, and still yet another, and so and so forth. Each universe is separated from the other by perpetual complete darkness so much so that the light of the sun, moon and stars is completely shut off. This immensely thick and equally immense wide band of darkness separates one universe from the other. No wonder therefore that Buddhism neither affirms nor denies the existence of a Supreme Creator, the God Almighty, whom one cannot see, feel or perceive while the Law of Karma furnishes demonstrable evidence in support of the theory of cosmology.

Each universe rests on a huge immense chunk of ether upon which rests the body of outer ocean which in turn supports a stratum of air or ether. To put in occult terms, the Oceans are Subtle and the Mountains are Gross, the one alternating with the other as Opposites. While the Central Enchanted Ocean is 80,000 miles deep and wide, "the succeeding girdle of Golden Mountains is half that number of miles in height, width and depth. The consecutive circles of alternating pairs comprised of Golden Mountains and Enchanted Ocean gradually diminish in width, depth and height, being respectively 20,000, 10,000, 5,000, 2,500, 1,250, and 625 miles. This brings us to the Continents in the Outer Ocean of Space." Of these Continents, the four chief ones are situated in the four directions. On either side of each of these four are smaller or satellite continents thus making a total of twelve, which again, is a symbolical number, like the number seven of the cosmographical arrangement.[4]

Violating the sanctity of sacred places can lead to serious consequences as is illustrated by the expedition of Laurens Van Der Posts in search of the vanished Bushmen of South Africa. His guide offered to take him to a place – Slippery Hills — where he might find what he was looking for. The guide laid down one condition that must be observed – there must be no killing whatsoever as they approached the site, otherwise the gods would be very angry. Unfortunately for Vender Post, he forgot to inform his advance party of this stipulation and one member of the team shot a warthog. An endless series of misfortune followed the incident. They were attacked by bees; the camera jammed continuously; when the guide to pray in a sacred place, something pulled him over backwards. The jamming of gadgets continued and another attack of bees took place. On consulting the spirits the guide was informed that the spirits were angry because they were approached with blood on their hands. The spirits told the guide that they would kill him if he tried to pray again. On this Vander Post suggested that they sign a letter of apology to the spirits, put the same in a bottle and place it at the foot of the Hill. This was done as planned. The Guide consulted the spirits again and they informed him that all would be well warning that when Vender Post would reach the next place on his itinerary, he would find bad news. So he did. A letter informed him that his father had died ten days earlier – on the day of sacrilege of the sacred Hill – and advised him to return home immediately.

A woman travelling by train on her way to consult a doctor for her stomach pains fell in conversation with a passenger who introduced himself as a healer and homeopath. Somehow he prevailed upon her to accept his invitation to join him for coffee. He suddenly took hold of her hand and she felt weak, dizzy with no will of her own. The man, Franz Walter, took her to a room in Heidelberg, placed her in a trance by placing his hand over her forehead and had intercourse with her. He exercised such power over her that she gave away her savings and prostituted herself for his benefit. Things came to such a pass that, under hypnotic influence, she agreed to murder her husband and made many attempts towards that end. But the husband became suspicious, reported the matter to the police and the police psychiatrist, Dr. Ludwig Mayer had the interesting task of somehow by-passing the complex system of hypnotic commands to the women. It became a notorious criminal case in a Heidelberg court in 1934 where Walter was sentenced to ten years imprisonment.

There is no end to the power of Evil!

The Tibetan Book of the Dead contains detailed instructions regarding the symptoms of death, besides actions to be taken by the priest(s) and the household to ensure that the departing body recognises and understands the significance of the Primary Clear Light at the of death. When the expiration has ceased, the vital force would have sunk into the nerve-center of Wisdom – a psychic nerve-center located in the heart region. In this state, the Knower would experience the Clear Light. Now is the time for the departing spirit to seek the path in Reality. The Guru informs the dying person of his situation. The throbbing of the arteries on the left and right side of the throat becomes pronounced, so these are pressed according to directions of the Guru. "At this moment, the first glimpsing of the Bardo of Clear Light of Reality, which is the Infallible Mind of Dharma-Kaya, is experienced by all sentient beings." The Guru keeps on repeating his advice until a yellowish liquid begins to ooze out from all apertures of the deceased.

Now comes the second stage: The Secondary Clear Light is seen immediately After Death. This is followed by the Third Stage of the Bardo when the Karmic Apparitions appear. The peaceful deities appear from the first to the seventh day after death. Then the wrathful deities make their appearance from the eighth to the fourteenth day after death.

THE PROCESS OF REBIRTH

The thought process of the dying person, immediately preceding actual death is a major contributory factor in determining the type of rebirth, parentage, family and social environment of the next life, etc. In some exceptional cases a person may be reborn in the same family as was in the case of little brother of His Holiness the Dalai Lama.[60] An ancestor generally takes rebirth in the same family environment – that is the belief amongst the communities of Canadian Northwestern territories who further believe that reincarnation must take place within one year of death, while the Buddhist belief system merely gives a time gap of forty-nine days only.

The soul hovers for about four days or so around the house where the body died. It is said to be on the lookout for a suitable womb where it might prefer to take rebirth.

Conclusion

Teachings of Bardo are of fundamental importance in Buddhism. Great Liberation by Hearing the fundamental teachings of the Bardo merely by hearing is possible even for those who have committed one or more of the following heinous sins: patricide, matricide, instigating two religious bodies at war, killing a saint, causing blood to flow from the body of a Tathagata (Buddha). Of course the Thodol is supreme for all since the real truth dawns on those who have mediated much during their life time as soon as the body and consciousness-principle get separated. It is therefore important that necessary experience is acquired while living in life. They obtain great power during the Bardo of the Moments of Death when the Clear Light appears around them.

Meditation is the essence of peaceful and complete liberation from this mortal world. Meditation on the mystic deities of the Mystic Path of the Mantra, visualising and the perfecting stages, while living, would be of great value when the peaceful and wrathful apparitions appear during the Third stage of Bardo. Therefore, training in this Bardo is of particular significance during a being's lifetime. It should be read at the side of all corpses. Spread and broadcast this Doctrine.

References

1. Evans-Wentz op. cit. p. 18.
2. *Ibid.*, p. 24.
3. *Ibid.*, p. 58.
4. Evan Wentz: op. cit. p. 64: Bulk of the foregoing data and descriptions are based on the text material in the Second Book of *Bàrdo Thödol*.
5. Gulati Mahinder: *REINCARNATION, A Recurring Cycle*; USA, 2008; p. 226.

   Butler, Tom and Lisa: There is No Death and there are No Dead; Reno, AA-EVP, 2003.

26

Liquor Drinking Gods

Spirits Love Spirit

Spirits do many strange things. If they want alcoholic drink they will find the bottle and take a drink, or anything else for that matter. The case of Malidoma Patrice Some of West African Dagara Tradition is well documented. He enjoyed his drink after the day's work. When he got home in the evening the first thing he looked for was his bottle of vodka simply because whenever the spirit(s) Kontombili showed up in the house they would finish off his bottle. As a matter of routine he brought home a bottle of vodka and placed the full bottle in the shrine, liquor-level at the top. By the morning the level in the bottle was down and next day it would be completely empty. Often Malidoma placed a bottle of liquor in the cave where the spirits dwelt and sooner rather than later the bottle just floated off and disappears! Unbelievable, but recorded as the truth!

Celebration of Holi is incomplete without gaiety and abandon that come with abundant alcohol, a classic example of alcohol and colour combining as depressant of central nervous system. However, it is not so amongst the Spirits in the spirit-world. Indeed Spirits love Spirit! Indian gods are not the only ones who enjoy their drink;

spirits in many other cultures also love to enjoy the taste of alcohol. The Old Testament has numerous references to drinking and making of wines. Alcohol was consumed in large quantities in Greek and Roman civilisations, by the rich and poor, by the gods in myths and legends. In Europe beers and wines were consumed in lieu of water which was often polluted. Early American settlers found it cumbersome to cart large containers of wines and beers so they resorted to making whisky from corn. Oriental cultures were no exception either. In Hindu classics there are numerous references to drinking of wines they called "*Sômç Rmss*". Saints, gods and general public enjoyed this alcoholic drink. The Arabs too distilled alcohol for personal consumption. Alcohol in one form or the other has long been used for medicinal purposes in surgery, childbirth, as an anesthetic, etc. since ancient times. Ancient Vedic culture was known for using mild alcoholic preparations for conducting religious ceremonies. So were the Greco-Roman cultures in which the wine-god (Dionysus or Bacchus) was most popular, more so since red wine symbolised the life blood of man. That is how Christianity came to acquire red wine for religious purification and rites of passage ceremonies — marriage, death, religious holidays, weekly Sabbath, circumcision, etc.

A man's capacity to drink liquor is limited. But the spirits have virtually unlimited capacity; they can drink any amount. You keep offering and they keep on drinking! That is precisely what happens to a dark-faced Indian god-idol in the Kaal Bhairav temple in UJJAIN, about fifty km from Indore. This famous temple was built by King Bhadresen on the bank of River Shirpa. There is an interesting mythological tale about River Shirpa. It is believed that the River had its origin in churning of the ocean by gods and demons using the serpent-god Vasuki as the rope. The ocean bed first yielded fourteen gems. Lakshmi, the Goddess of Wealth, came next followed by the coveted vessel containing the Nectar of Immortality which was picked up by the gods. The demons chased the gods and in the process a few drops of the precious nectar spilled over and fell at Ujjayini (modern Ujjain), Haridwar, Nasik and Prayag. Ujjain thus became one of the holiest cities of India situated in the state of Madhya Pradesh. Lord Shiva is the presiding deity of this holy city which was known as Avantipura in pre-historic times.

Ujjain lay on the main trade route between North India and Deccan. Starting from Mathura the route led to Ujjain and thence to Mahismati (Maheshwar) on the Narbada. The Northern Black Polished (NBP), the finest pottery of the time, thus found its way to South India and thence to Middle East. These included precious stones, pearls, scents, spices, perfumes, muslin and silks. After the Paramara sovereignty in the Malwa came to an end in 946 C.E. the capital was shifted to the Mahakala Vana area in Ujjain.

Ujjain is significant in more ways than one, besides of course being the abode of liquor drinking god Bhairav. The importance of Ujjain is enhanced for geographical and astronomical reasons also. The Tropic of Cancer is supposed to pass through Ujjain. It is also the first meridian of the longitude of Hindu geographers thereby enjoying the reputation of being 'India's Greenwich'. The temple of Mangainath is believed to be the birth place of Mars. It was well known for a clear view of planet Mars and hence suitable for astronomical studies. Two great works of astronomy, the *Surya Siddhanta* and *Panch Siddhanta* were written at Ujjain. During the reign of Mahmud Shah, Maharaja Sawai Jai Singh (1686-1743) was appointed Governor of Malwa. He was a great scholar of astronomy and had the Ujjain-observatory (*Vedha Shala*) reconstructed besides numerous temples.

The thousands of years old City is dotted with innumerable temples. Ujjain is considered one of the most sacred places where the Kumbha Mela is held once every twelve years. Every temple is sacred and notable in its own way; the Maha Kaal temple is the most sacred of all in which Bhairav gods are worshipped. There are eight Bhairav gods whose worship is part of the Shiite tradition; Kaal Bhairav is the chief among them. Every day hundreds and thousands of worshippers visit this famous temple and reverently offer bottles after bottle of raw country-liquor which the god just gobbles down. Amazing, but literally true! After all, there are ingenious ways of disposing off such offerings! ... In keeping with the tradition I too presented a bottle to the deity when we visited the place some years back. In fact rather than pilgrimage, curiosity was the sole reason for my visit to Ujjain.

Kaal Bhairav Temple (Bhaironath — the liquor drinking deity) is mentioned in the *Avanti Khand*a of ancient Indian scripture, the *Skanda Purana*. In fact, the *Puranas* are the main source of sacred geography of India. The temple priest keeps the 'dish' filled with country-liquor in front of mouth of the Deity. The stone image starts sucking the liquor slowly from the dish. When the plate is completely empty the priest takes it back. Sounds unbelievable but is certainly true, absolutely true at least for the eyes! This happens every day, many times a day. During the festival days the Deity sucks in hundreds of bottles in a day, but still remains sober! The god is never drunk!

Maha Shivratri is a major annual event. *Simhastha Kumbh* Mela is a mammoth gathering of pilgrims and worshippers held once every twelve years. Mahakaal is the presiding deity of Ujjain. It dominates the sacred city in its entirety. Of course other gods of Hindu pantheon are also well represented in the numerous temples that dot the countryside. However, Shiva reigns supreme in Ujjain. The worship of eight Bhairav is a part of Saivite tradition, the chief among them being Kaal Bhairav. Bhaironath *vahan* (vehicle) is the dog. Feeding and caring the dog(s) brings good karma to the devotee.

The idol of Mahakaleshwar is *dakshinamurti* i.e., facing south. This is a unique feature upheld by tantric tradition. *Bhasma Aarti* held at every dawn is the prime attraction. The master of cosmic time is propitiated with ash from the cremation ground. The ash is symbolic of the end of manifestation of existential time. It is noteworthy that in Ujjain's temple of liquor-drinking god only raw country-liquor is offered, and also served as Prasad. Other forms of Prasad are purely vegetarian. However, in the *Maa Olasuni* temple on a hillock in village Olasuni astride National Highway 5A in Orissa is an odd exception. Here not only raw country liquor but also refined India-made-foreign liquor is offered to the deity and as Prasad to the devotees. However, the most surprising practice in this Temple is that non-vegetarian items like meat, fish, chicken etc. are also offered to propitiate the deity. These non-vegetarian offerings are also consumed by the devotees as Prasad. Of course, beef is prohibited. This temple was established in the 17th century by Sant Arakhita Das in the dense forest at the Olasuni hillock. He was a strong believer in non-vegetarian food, and hence the customary Prasad.

References

1. Evans-Wentz op. cit. p. 18.
2. *Ibid.,* p. 24.
3. *Ibid.,* p. 58.
4. Evan Wentz: op. cit. p. 64: Bulk of the foregoing data and descriptions are based on the text material in the Second Book of *Bardo Thödol*.

27

Milk Drinking Gods

On the night of September 20/21, 1995 an ordinary Hindu devout citizen of South Delhi dreamt that Ganesha, the elephant-headed God of Wisdom, was craving for a little milk. Well before dawn he rushed to the nearest temple. It was not yet open. But the skeptical priest accepted his entreaties and allowed him to take a spoonful of milk to the mouth of the stone-idol. Both watched in astonishment and were totally flabbergasted when milk from the spoon just disappeared as if it was magically consumed by the God. What followed during the next few hours not only in India but all over the Hindu-world turned out to be "the best documented paranormal phenomenon of modern times", unprecedented in modern Hindu history.

Within hours the news spread like a bush-fire not only across the whole of India but also across the globe that God Ganesha was accepting milk offerings. Tens of millions of people of all ages flocked to thousands of temples all across the country carrying milk to feed the thirsty God. Delhi came to a standstill, so did many pockets of Hindu population in Britain, Canada, United States, Dubai, Nepal, Thailand, Hong Kong, Indonesia and other South East Asian counties. The world media went berserk. BBC, CNN, New York Times and all the prestigious news services picked up the story and flashed it across headlines. Not that they all believed it, but it was novelty and expression of faith of Hindu millions that no respectable news service wanted to be left behind.

Milk prices shot up. Soon milk was not available even to feed babies. Mass hysteria had gripped Delhi and metropolitan cities. *The Guardian* (London, September 21, 1995) reported: Life in India virtually came to a standstill! To cap it all, amazing manifestation of Divine power occurred in a Hindu temple in Wimbledon (South London) when milk offered to the God disappeared, and *Vibhuti* (holy ash) simultaneously appeared on forehead of Sai Baba and *amrit* (nectar) flowed from his feet.

The bubble burst as quickly as it had formed. Within twenty-four hours Lord Ganesha refused to accept milk. Millions of Hindus had missed the bus. The media continued to follow the story propounding many theories to explain the unheard of phenomenon with no apparent answer. Scientists were deputed from the Ministry of Science and Technology who offered milk with some food-coloring. The world of science would naturally not accept the version of blind-faith. The scientific explanation was capillary action and surface tension of milk pulling the liquid up and out of the spoon, while gravity took over causing the milk to spill down the stone idols. But there was hardly any rational explanation why had the phenomenon suddenly overtaken the Hindu masses, and why it had abruptly come to a standstill in India while it continued overseas for a few more days.

I do remember the morning of September 22, 1995... It was all so quiet!

It is noteworthy that capillary-action/surface-tension phenomenon had not been reported/observed at all during the past centuries and that it was limited to idols of Ganesha, Shiva and Durga only. When the 'miracle' occurred again on January 13/14, 2008 yet another explanation: The milk did not disappear; it was simply soaked up by the plaster of which the idols were made of !

Subsequently, a number of such interesting 'miracles' were reported from various parts of the country. The "Sai Baba '*chamatkârs*'" (miracles) are on top of the list. Details of innumerable chronic medical problems cured by the Baba through his 'super-natural' powers would perhaps fill a full volume. The smiling face of the Baba appearing in the rain soaked clouds was witnessed by one and all for which the electronic media takes the cake.

Amongst hundreds of purported 'miracles' for which the Baba is well known, the latest one is the statute of Shirdi Sai Baba in a merchant's house in Bangalore. The statute has opened its left eye, apparently like a real eye. Messages from the other world have been a pet research topic by many specialists in paranormal field. Edgar Cayce's and Dr. Brian Weiss's voluminous works, and of many others too, have given authoritative proof of communication between the departed loved ones to their loved ones left behind. The latest is Stephen Wagner's compilation citing "compelling anecdotal evidence of life after death" in the form of messages from deceased loved ones. The Shamans' journeys to the "*land of the dead*" are exactly what all this is about.

Following reports of a picture of Jesus Christ "bleeding" from the heart", the "Bleeding Christ" in cosmopolitan Bombay where thousands of believers flocked to St Michael's Church. Further, the electronic media gave wide coverage to Guru Gobind Singh's pet bird and messenger, *BÂJ* (hawk), pecking at the picture of the Guru in the Amritsar Gurdwara for almost three days at a stretch.

The foregoing instances naturally took my mind back to the French Lady David Neel Alexandria's experiences in Tibet. This remarkable woman, Louis Eugene Alexandra Marie David was the first and the only female European Lama in Tibetan hierarchy. She entered Tibet for the first time in 1916 but had to return to Sikkim under orders of the authorities of British India. Her indomitable spirit took her from Sikkim to Japan-China thence to (Tibetan) Kumbum Monastery in Eastern China where she spent more than two years. During this period the Monastery ran short of supplies. David Neel gave her own money to her helper to procure supplies and bring them over in a caravan of mules. Everyone in the monastery was anxiously awaiting the arrival of her helper leading the caravan of much needed supplies. It was late evening when they all saw the man and the caravan coming up the steep mountain path. But it soon disappeared before their very eyes. The search parties just could not find any trace of the man with the hat and his caravan of animals laden with supplies. The most interesting part of the episode was that the same caravan with the same leader in exactly the same dress wearing the same characteristic hat leading the caravan was again seen on the same path the next evening. And that was indeed real in flesh and bones — Mind does play games with reason and intellect!

It is all a matter of faith. There are many gaps in the scientific explanation offered as there are in the versions of believers.— No wonder therefore that Christians the world over would be prepared to shed blood against blasphemy if someone ever suggested that Jesus had married a sex-worker. Mary Magdalene and had two children from her; or that the original Virgin Mary was Jesus's wife and not his mother .The 1500-years old manuscript, *'Lost Gospel'* painstakingly translated from Aramic, by a Professor Barrie Wilson and writer Simcha

Jacobovic make no bones about making these revelation-allegations were earlier made by Don Brown in *'The Da Vinci code' besides the 1953-Book, 'The last temptation of Christ'* by Nikos Kazantzakis. In this context it is rather strange, and suspicious too, that the Canonical Gospels, after mentioning the birth of Jesus, and then narrate his visit with his parents to the temple of Jerusalem by which time He was just about twelve years of age. "The Gospels than suddenly introduce him at his thirtieth year, and are absolutely silent about the intervening period covering eighteen or more years. They tell us nothing about his youth, his habits, education or occupation, nor about his years in India, his death and burial in Srinagar.

According to the Gospels, we next find Jesus in the desert till the day of his showing into Israel before which He spent a few years in Nepal from where. He travelled through Kashmir, Afghanistan and Persia.

References

1. The times of India, Dehradun edition, 11 Nov. 2014.
2. Khwaja Nazir Ahmad: *JESUS in Heaven on Earth (Journey of Jesus to Kashmir, his preaching to the Lost Tribes of Israel and his death and burial in Srinagar); Ammadiyya Anjuman Isha'at Lahore Inc. USA, 1998; P. Isha'at Lahore Inc. USA, 1998; pp. 53,355.*

Bibliography

Adam Crabtree: *Multiple Man: Explorations in Possessions and* Ake Hultkrantz: *The Religion of the American Indians*; 1967/1979.

Albert Taylor: *Soul Traveler*; New York, 1998.

Andrew Greeley: *Mysticism Goes Mainstream*, 1982.

Andrew MacKenzie: *Haunting and Apparitions*; London 1982.

Annie Besant and C.W. Leadbeater: *Thought-Forms*, Wheaton, 1925.

Anthony Finlay: Demons! *The Devil, Possession and Exorcism*; Blandford, UK, 1999.

Barbanell Maurice: *This is Spiritualism*; Spiritualism Press, USA, 1959.

Barrett William; *Death-Bed Visions: The Psychical Experience of the Dying*; England, 1926.

Benjamin B. Wolman, ed. *Handbook of Parapsychology*; New York, 1977.

Bill Guggenheim and Judy Guggenheim: *HELLO FROM HEAVEN*.

Bantam Book, New York, 1995; paperback edition April 1997.

Bill School: *The Psychic Powers of Animals*; New York, 1977.

Blavatsky H.P.: *Isis Unveiled: A Master Key to the Mysteries of Ancient and Modern Science and Theology*; London and Benares, The Theosophical Publishing Society, 1910.

Blavatsky H.P.: *The Secret Doctrine*; New York, 1907.

Bletzer, June G.: *The Encyclopedia Psychic Dictionary*; Lithia Springs, New Leaf, 1998.

Boone Allen Jones: *Kinship with all Life*; New York, Harper and Row, 1954.

Brennan J.H.: *Magical Techniques of Tibet*; New Age Books, New Delhi, 2003.

Occult Tibet, Secret Practices of Himalayan Magic, Llewewelln Publications,USA, 2002.

Brian Weiss, Dr.: *Same Soul, Many Bodies*; Piatkus 2004.

Many Lives, Many Masters.

Messages from the Masters.

Bruce Goldberg: *Past Lives, Future Lives*; New York, 1982.

Bruce Kraig: *The Stonehenge: The Indo-European Heritage*; Chicago, 1978.

Buckland Raymond: *The Encyclopedia of Divination and* Butler, Tom and Lisa: *There is No Death and There are No Dead*; Reno, AA-EVP, 2003.

Cavendish Richard (ed.): *Man, Myth and Magic: An Encyclopedia of the Supernatural*; London, BPC, 1970.

C.E. Green: *Lucid Dreams*, London, 1968.

C.G. Jung: *Dreams*; Princeton, 1974.

C.G. Jung: *Man His Symbols*, 1964;

Celia Green: Apparitions, London, 1975.

Charles Berlitz: *Atlantis, the Eighth Continent*; New York, 1984.

Charles Berlitz: *The Bermuda Triangle*; New York, 1974 *Without a Trace* New York 1977.

Charles Emmons; *Chinese Ghosts and ESP*, NJ.

Chogyam Trungpa; Shambhala: *The Sacred Path of the Warrior*, 1984; New York 1986.

Christopher Chippindale: *Stonehenge Complete,* New York, 1983.

Christoph von Haimendorf: *Himalayan Barbarity*; John Murray, London 1955.

Cllin Wilson: *Mysteries*; Watkin Publishing, London, 2006.

Mysteries; New York, 1978.

The psychic Detectives; San Francisco, 1985.

The Psychic Detectives; San Francisco, 1985.

Dalai Lama, His Holiness: My Land and My People; Srishti Publishers, 1977.

The Transformed Mind; Coronet Books; Penguin, 1999.

David Jones: *Visions: of Time; Experiments in Psychic Archeology*; IL, 1979.

David Smith: *Hinduism and Modernity*; Blackwell Publishing, 2003.

David-Neel Alexandra: *Magic and Mystery in Tibet*; Dover Publications, New York, 1965.

My Journey to Lhasa; Boston, 1986.

Bandits, Priests and Demons; The Hague; 1988.

Initiations and Initiates in Tibet; Rider, London, 1970.

Dona Zohar: *Through the Time Barrier; A Study in Precognition and Modern Physics*.

Doyle, Sir Arthur Conan: *The History of Spiritualism*; New York, Doran, 1926.

Echo Bodine: *Relax It's Only a GHOST*; Element, Boston, 2000.

Edgar D. Mitchell: *Psychic Exploration: A Challenge For Science*, New York 1974.

Edger Cayce *on Atlantis*, New York 1968.

Edger D. Mitchell: *Psychic Exploration, A Challenge for Science*, New York, 1974.

Edmund Gurney: *Phantasms of the Living*, London, 1886.

Edwin Bernbaum: *The Way to Shambhala*; New York, 1980.

Elizabeth E. McAdams: *The Case for Life After Death*, Chicago, 1981.

Emmons Charles: *Chinese Ghosts and ESP*, New Jersey.

Evans-Pritchard, E.E.; *Witchcraft, Oracles, and Magic among the Azande*, Clarden Press, Oxford, 1937

Evan Wentz W.Y.: *Thought-Forms*; 1954.

The Tibetan Book of the Great Liberation; London, 1954.

The Tibetan Book of the Dead; London, 1960.

Tibetan Yoga and Secret Doctrines; Oxford University Press, 1969

The Spirit Book Extracts from edger Cayce Readings: Virginia Beach, VA;

Edger Cayce Foundation, 1976.

Fodor, Nandor: *Encyclopedia of Psychic Science*; London, Arthur Press, 1933.

Fortune Dion: *Psychic Self Defence*, York Beach; 1930.

Francis King: *Tantra for Westerners*; The Aquarian Press, Welling Brough; 1986.

Frank Podmore: *Phantoms of the Living*; London 1886.

Frederic Bligh Bond: *The Gate of Remembrance*, Oxford, 1921.

Frederick Lenz: *True Accounts of Reincarnation*; New York, 1977.

Fredrick W.H. Myers: *Human Personality and Its Survival After Death*; Vol I and II; 1903.

George ANDERSON'S Conversations with the Other Side, Berkley Books, New York, 1989.

George W. Meak: *Healers and the Healing Process*; Wheaton, 1977.

Gerald S. Hawkins: *Beyond Stonehenge*; New York, 1973.

Geraldine Cummins: *Unseen Adventures*; London, 1951.

GNM Tyrell: *Apparitions*, 1943.

Green C.E.: *Lucid Dreams*, 1968, London.

Guiley Rosemary Ellen: *Encyclopedia OF THE STRANGE, Harper's Encyclopedia of Mystical and Paranormal Experience*, San Francisco,1991.

The Encyclopedia of Ghosts and Spirits; New York, Facts on File, 1992.

Gulati M.N.: *Enigmatic Tibet*; Manas Publications, New Delhi, 2005.

Gulati N. Mahinder: *Worlds Youngest Religion: SIKHISM: Islamic Influence and Tibetan Connection*; Atlantic Publishers, New Delhi.

Gurney Edmunds: *Phantoms of the Living*; London 1886.

H.P. Blavatsky: *The Secret Doctrine*; New York, 1907.

Harold Sherman: *Wonder Healers of the Philippines*; LA, 1967.

Harpers Encyclopedia Mystical and Paranormal Experiences, 1991, San Francisco.

Henry Griss: *The New Soviet Psychic Discoveries*, New Jersey, 1978.

Herbert B. Greenhouse: *Premonition, A Leap into the Future*; New York 1971.

Hornell Hart: *The Enigma of Survival*, Springfield.

James Churchward: *The Children of Mu*; New York, 1931.

Jane Roberts: *Adventures in Consciousness*, New York, 1979. *The Nature of Personal Reality*, NJ, 1974.

Jeffrey Goodman: *Psychic Archaeology: Time Machine to the Past*; New York, 1977.

Joel Martin and Patricia Romanowski: *WE DON'T DIE: George Anderson's Conversations with the Other Side.*

Joel Whitton: *Life Between Life.*

John A. Sanford: Dreams: *God's Forgotten Language*, San Francisco, 1968.

John Ferguson: *An Illustrated Encyclopedia of Mysticism and Mystery Religions*: New York 1976.

John G. Fuller: *Arigo: Surgeon of the Rusty Knife*; New York 1974.

Jon Klimo: *Channeling: Investigations on Receiving Information from Paranormal Sources*; Los Angeles, 1987.

Jonathan Adolph: *Shaman*; Beverly Hills.

Jonathan Cott: *The Search for Om Sety*; New York, 1987.

Jung C.G.: *Dreams*, Princeton, 1974 *Man and His Symbols*, 1964.

Karkis Osis: *Deathbed Observations by Physicians and Nurses*; New York, 1961.

Keith Harary, Dr: *Out of Body Experiences.*

Keith Thomas: *Religion and Decline of Magic*, New York, 1971.

Kenneth Ring: *Heading Towards Omega*, New York, 1984.

Lawrence David Kusche: *The Bermuda Triangle Mystery Solved*; New York, 1975.

Life at Death: A Scientific Investigation of NDE Experience, New York, 1980.

Lord Auerbach: *ESP, Hauntings and Poltergeists*, New York, 1986.

Louisa E. Rhine: *Mind Over Matter: Psychokinesis*; New York, 1970. *ESP in Life and Lab*, New York, 1967.

Lyall Watson: *Beyond Supernature*; New York, 1987.

Lynn V. Andrews: *We are made from Stars and to the Stars We must Return*, New York, Warner Books, 1986.

Mahinder Gulati: *Reincarnation: A Recurring Cycle*; Xlibris, Philadelphia, 2008.

Merlin Stone: *When God was a Woman*, San Diego, 1976.

Michael Harner: *The way of the Shaman*; New York, 1986.

Michael Loewe: *Oracles and Divination*, Borders, Shambhala, 1981.

Michael Newton: *Journey of Souls*.

Mircea Eliade: *Shamanism*; New Jersey 1951; Princeton, 1964.

Monica Furlong: *Zen Effects: The Life of Adam Watts*; New York, 1986. *Selected Writings of Gopi Krishna*.

Moody Dr. Raymond A: *Life After Life*, New York, 1975.

Morton Kelsey: *Dreams, A Way to Listen to God*, 1978.

Multiple Personality; New York 1985

MYSTICAL and UNEXPLAINED; 1991, Random House, New York.

Nicholas Negush: *The Human Aura*; New York, 1974.

Noel Langley: *Edger Cayce on Reincarnation*; New York, Castle Books, 1967.

Norma Lee Browning: Peter Hurkos: *I have Many Lives*; New York 1976.

Ormond McGill: *The Mysticism and Magic of India*, New Jersey, 1977.

Oscar Bagnall: *The Properties of the Human Aura*; New York 1970.

Pandit Shriram Sharma Acharya: *Extra Sensory Potential of the Mind*; Shri Vedmata Gyatri Trust, 2001, Haridwar.

Patricia L. Garfield: *Creative Dreaming*, New York, 1972.

Paul Tabori: *Crime and the Occult*; New York, 1974.

Philosophy and Religion of Spiritualism; Milwaukee, Morris Pratt Institute, 1973.

Psychical Research: *A Survey and Tentative Interpretation of* Avialable Findings *from Nina Kuagina and Other Known Related Cases of Recent Date*; Jan 1976.

Radhakrishnan S.: *The Principal Upanisads*; HarperCollins 1994.

Raymond Buckland: *The Spirit Book, The Encyclopedia of Clairvoyance, Channeling, And Spirit Communication*, Canton, USA, 2005.

Reliving Past Lives; New York, 1978.

Rev. Carroll E. Jay: *Gretchen, I Am*; New York 1977.

Rhine J.B.: *The Reach of the Mind*; New York, 1947.

Richard Smoley: *Inner Christianity: A guide to the Esoteric Traditions*; Shambhala, 2002.

Robert A. Johnson: *Inner Work*, New York, 1986.

Robert Monroe: *Ultimate Journey*.

Robert O. Becker: *The Body Electric; Electromagnetism and the Foundation of Life*; New York, 1985.

Rogo Scott D.: *Psychic Breakthroughs Today*; England 1987.

Rudolf Steiner: *The Cosmic Memory*; San Francisco, 1959.

Rustie Brown: *The Titanic, The Psychic and the Sea*, California, 1981.

Ruth Montgomery: *A Search for the Truth*.

Shafica Karagulla: *The Chakras and the Human Energy Fields.*

Sheila Ostrander and Lynn Schroeder: *Psychic Discoveries Behind the Iron Curtain*; Englewood Cliffs, NJ; Prentice-Hall, 1970.

Sherman, Harold: *You Can Communicate With the Unseen World*; New York, Fawcett, 1974.

Shirley MacLaine: *Out on a Limb*; *A Course in Miracles* — Foundation for Inner Peace.

Sigmund Freud: *The Interpretation of Dreams*, New York, 1900.

Soothsaying; Detroit, Visible Ink Press, 2004.

Stanley Krippner: *The Realms of Healing*; Berkley, 1986.

Stephen A. Schwartz: *The Alexandria Project*, New York 1983.

Stephen LaBerge: *Lucid Dreaming*, New York, 1985.

Stevenson Ian Pretyman, Dr.: *Reincarnation and Biology: A Contribution to the Etiology of Birthmarks and Birth Defects; Twenty Cases Suggestive of Reincarnation* (1966) *Where Reincarnation and Biology Intersect* (1977).

Sture Lunnerstrand (Author), Leslie Kippen (Translator) *I Have Lived Before: The True Story of Reincarnation of Shanti Devi,* Ozark Mountain Publishing, 1998.

Tribal Transformation in India Volume V – *Religion Rituals and Festivals*; EE Buddhadeb Chaudhuri; Inter-India Publications, New Delhi, 1992.

Unlearned Language: New Studies in Xenoglossy, 1974 India: *Cases of the Reincarnation Type*; 1975.

Walter J. Kilner: *The Human Aura*; New York, 1920.

Whitney S. Hibbard: *Psychic Criminology: An Operations Manual for Using Psychics in Criminal Investigations*, Springfield; 1982.

William Flexner: *An Introduction to Parapsycholgy*; Sarup and Sons; 2004.

William H. Kautz: *Channeling: The Intuitive Connection*; San Francisco, 1987.

William James: *The Varieties of Religious Experience*; New York, 1902.

Zaleski Carol: *Other World Journeys: Accounts of NDE in Medieval and Modern Times*, New York, 1987.

Index

K

L

M

N

O

P

R

V

W

X

Y

Z